CLASSIC *f*M

GARDEN PLANNER

STEFAN BUCZACKI
FRED DOWNHAM
SUE PHILLIPS
with
DAPHNE LEDWARD

THE GARDENING FORUM TEAM

PAVILION

First published in Great Britain in 1996 by
PAVILION BOOKS LIMITED
26 Upper Ground, London SE1 9PD

Text copyright © Stefan Buczacki, Fred Downham,
Daphne Ledward and Sue Phillips 1996
Line drawings copyright © Will Giles and Sandra Pond 1996
Colour illustrations copyright © Nadine Wickenden 1996
Photographs copyright ©Andrew Lawson (jacket, pp 10, 14, 54, 107, 130);
© Garden Picture Library Steven Wooster (p 2);
© Jerry Harpur (pp 34, 50, 79, 90, 122);
© Photos Horticultural (p 150)

Designed by The Bridgewater Book Company

A CIP catalogue record for this book is available from the British Library

ISBN 1 85793 664 7

Printed and bound in Dubai

2 4 6 8 10 9 7 5 3 1

This book may be ordered by post direct from the publisher. Please contact the
Marketing Department. But try your bookshop first.

CLASSIC *f*M

GARDEN

PLANNER

Contents

— 6 —

INTRODUCTION

— 10 —

SPRING

— 50 —

SUMMER

— 90 —

AUTUMN

— 130 —

WINTER

— 172 —

APPENDIX

— 176 —

INDEX

INTRODUCTION

SOONER OR LATER, anyone who earns their living by writing gardening books and articles (or making gardening programmes) will be asked the same question: 'Don't you find that you are repeating yourself?' It's a fair enough query, for the fact that gardening is a cyclic activity is self-evident. Summer follows spring, warmth follows frost, fruits and seeds follow flowers as certainly as anything in nature. So, surely, the gardening advice that is given in March this year will be the same as that given in March last year and so on back to the misty origins of horticulture. And surely too, the advice given in this book or magazine is much the same as that in any other.

No, I must dispute much of this (but then he would say that, wouldn't he?). This is not because of our need for continuing employment but simply because no one gardens for very long before they discover that no two seasons are ever the same. And I long ago realized that calendar months aren't of much value as signposts to gardening activity. It is nature, not the mathematical calculation of diarists, that dictates when things should be done. The onset and end of the season's frosts in your particular part of the country are the most important guides to when gardening should be planned. Besides, gardening as we have to consider it is such a vast topic — ranging from the provision of electricity for a greenhouse to the control of groundsel, with every gardener having his or her own favourite ways of doing each task — that the possibilities and permutations must be endless.

And how fortunate we all are to garden in a country that offers a greater combination of soils and weather than can be found in any other area of comparable size anywhere else in the world, while lacking those real climatic extremes. It is this ideal gardening environment, together with the endeavours of the many plant collectors who have left these islands to send back specimens from every corner of the globe, that has yielded such a dazzling variety of planting in such a dazzling variety of gardens.

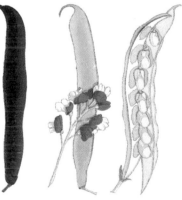

I can remember as if it was yesterday the behaviour of a French friend paying his first visit to Britain many years ago. I was giving him his first conducted tour around my garden. No sooner had we set foot upon the lawn than he dropped to his knees, rather in the manner that hallowed that it justified being kissed, so it was with some relief that my friend explained that he was only taking a close look at what, for any foreigner, is the cream of a British garden – the grass. We have grass like no one else's, I was told, and I am inclined to think he could be right. Certainly it is often grass rather than gravel, stone or statuary that gives the British garden much of its individuality, but I can think of many gardens in this country so emphatically stamped with a national identity (be it embodied in grass or some other feature) that they could not possibly be anywhere else on earth.

To say merely that the British garden is eclectic is a simplification, for like so many facets of our national life, what has come to be marked so indelibly as 'British' is in fact a pot pourri of influences, styles, fashions and ingredients from far and wide. And although we often talk glibly of the British gardening style, I can think of very few of our gardens that are of wholly indigenous construction and inspiration. They have collected influences from Italian formality, French flair, Dutch regimentation and Oriental symbolism. And they look so very different. They range from the geometric regularity of the medieval through the timeless informality of the cottage garden and William Robinson's 'wild' approach to the more modern disciplines of Jekyll and the late twentieth-century concept of the outdoor room.

Yes, someone once described us as a nation of gardeners. The more I travel in this country, the more I see the truth of this. There is undeniably a vast wealth of good, much very good and some very great gardening in Britain. There is a breadth and a depth, too, of gardening knowledge among all strata of society. It would be facile to say this is because over the centuries we have copied each and every fashion and trend that happened along. Equally, it could be because we have had the wit to learn, to analyse, appraise, and both to reject and to retain with discernment, thus producing in the end something of uniquely special and enduring quality. I choose to think the latter; and I think that our gardens themselves prove me right.

Hence, in a sense, this book. Collectively, we must have in excess of one hundred and twenty-five years of gardening experience, as well as over forty of broadcasting. There is no corner of the British Isles that we haven't visited, no type of garden that we haven't seen and yet every programme that we make is markedly distinct. No two answers are ever the same (even to the same question) and most assuredly no two audiences and no two venues are ever remotely similar. So we have drawn on our collective experiences to write this journal, not as a blueprint to be followed slavishly, for gardening is not like that, but to serve as a reminder, as something to point you in particular directions and give you topics to contemplate. I hope it will be a book for every season and will be your companion in your garden and as you listen to our programmes. Let us know if you enjoy it, let us know if you agree or disagree with our ideas and suggestions. We want you to be a part of Classic Gardening Forum. SB

Spring

THERE ARE FEW things in life's experience to match our land and our gardens in spring. As soon as we turn February's cold and dismal corner, there will be promises, hints and tantalizing glimpses of the splendour that is to come. Not every day, not for a while yet, but in my garden it first appears in the form of the early crocuses that brave the wind and rain, to be followed in time by my ever-faithful daffodils. Nothing keeps them down for long and once I have seen good 'King Alfred' show his golden crown, I know that tulips will follow and that my garden is truly alive again.

But no gardener's time is ever spent very long in mere admiration of his or her efforts. Good gardens may sometimes happen by accident, but most are the result of a certain amount of planning and hard work. Many of those bulbs, for instance, now giving such excellent displays will gradually fade away in years to come unless they are given the wherewithal to build up their food reserves anew. As soon as the flowers fade, therefore, remove as many as possible of the dead blooms and begin to give the foliage a fortnightly treat of liquid fertilizer for about six weeks.

Spring is, of course, also seed-sowing time – at first indoors but later, as the soil warms up, outside too. The timings on your seed packet can be telescoped by the judicious use of cloches which will enable you to pre-warm the soil and thus help seeds to germinate more quickly and surely. And as the seedlings emerge, the cloches can remain in position and so allow our unpredictable weather to give rather less of a shock to tender young things having their first glimpse of the great outdoors. But for those who prefer to have their young plants ready-made, the watchword here must be one of caution: even in the world of today's generally high horticultural standards, I see still young plants raised in the warmth of a greenhouse and then abruptly thrust on to cold and draughty pavements and shop counters. Do be sure that your youngsters have been hardened off. *SB*

NOTES 8/3/97.

Ali laid out beds for sowing 10
beds, garlic & onion already sown.
Herb garden already mint, coriander, lemon
Thyme and chives. Greenhouse built
recently. Sowing started. ——————
FROST - heater on overnight.   Cat
                                                Eated
                                                grass.

9/3/97 - Sunday. Heater on Night time vents on
propagator closed. nights., put on ground. Scoot
Trays wet - didn't water. - put on Table. Grass.

10/3/97 - Monday. night - heater on.   warm
                                               Day.

Leaf salads are
tremendously productive
as there is no need to wait
till individual crops
mature. Start using the
thinnings as soon as the
seedlings begin to show
some leaf. Keep thinning
until the remaining plants
are well spaced out, then
leave them to mature
partly or fully.

11/3/97 - Tuesday. Watered. Warm
      Heater on.   Day.

12/3/97 - Trays wet. Watered Garlic/Onions

13/3/97 - No Heater

14/3/97 - Watered All.

16/3/97. Watered All. Seedlings
                          Nightstock + lettuce

NB. POTATOES.

EARTH UP.	
Pots.	3
Ground	4
Grow	5
Fertilizer	2
Ground	1

17/3/97 - PLANT Seed - Cauliflower + Tomato
      ½ pkt each. Watered.
      Heater On.   Tony's sweetpeas
                                        in.!

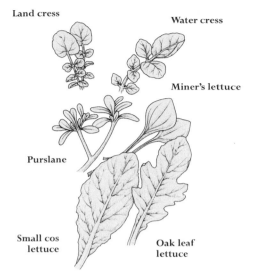

Land cress

Water cress

Miner's lettuce

Purslane

Small cos lettuce

Oak leaf lettuce

SALAD LEAVES FOR SPRING

GREEN SALADS are the gourmet equivalent of the little black dress – handy for any occasion. And you don't need much space to grow your own ingredients.

Start in spring by preparing the ground well: fork in lots of moisture-retaining compost, sprinkle a handful of blood, fish and bone fertilizer per square metre or yard, and rake to a fine tilth. Then sow a few seeds of each of lots of different salad leaves. Sow in separate rows a hoe's width apart for easy weeding, or, on really weed-free soil, mix everything together and scatter randomly.

I like a selection of lettuce – mini cos 'Little Gem', tiny hearting 'Tom Thumb' and several pretty oak-leaved and frilly red varieties – plus chicory, raddichio and endive. (Though normally sown much later for winter hearts, their young leaves add useful colours, textures and flavours to salads.) For added 'bite', include salad onions, peppery rocket and land cress, plus claytonia and purslane for their thick succulent leaves. Leafy herbs like dill, coriander, parsley, leaf celery, borage and chervil are good, too. Sow salad leaves every four weeks to be sure of a constant supply, and vary the mix through the season. Half-hardy kinds of salad like purslane and some herbs should not be sown till after the last frost; add Chinese cabbage and other oriental leaves from mid June onwards. *SP*

19/3/97 – Watered.

22/3/97 FROST.

23/3/97 – Plant in smaller Trays Toms + Cauliflower seeds. 1 Sage appears.

26/3/97 – Cuthberts CABBAGE (Greyhound) in watered paper in flat tub. put in front Cubbord + brown paper.
" Cabbage " — seeds
Sown Greenhouse - 2 Pots +2 Modules
CARROT - Autumn 1 Pots King 2 2? Modules
Watered All. Heater on.

27/3/96 – Plant Herbs. 10 assorted. Water butt fixed.

28/3/97 – Rocket Planted rows + rockery

29/3/96. Pricked Out lettuce into ~4 Modules
Sowed 1 Mod. Beetroot 1/2 pkt.
" " " " covered Brussel Sprouts 1 pkt.

Heater on early.

1/4/97 Tuesday. Pricked out Cauliflower (2 Modul?
Sage - (1 Module) Lettuce now = 4 Modules.
Parsley shoots in ground. Cabbage seed in smal
shoot
Module.
SweetCorn 12 pts Planted in 2in. Pots.
Peas - planted outside, Blk. thrd. protected.
Dill - outside + 1 seed tray.
Night stock Seeds in behind Roses. etc.
Camomile Lawn,

CLASSIC CLIMBER

CLEMATIS ARMANDII

Climbers which flower early in the year are very desirable, and if they happen to have evergreen leaves, and fragrance as well, so much the better. *Clematis armandii* is one such rare treasure.

Discovered in China at the turn of the century, it is the hardiest of around eighteen evergreen species of clematis. *C. armandii* is almost worth growing for its spectacular leathery, dark green leaves alone, but add to

this a profusion of small white or creamy-white, four- or six-petalled flowers with a delicate vanilla fragrance, and you have the perfect climbing plant to brighten the spring.

Two named varieties are 'Apple Blossom' and 'Snowdrift'. The flowers of 'Apple Blossom' are 5–6cm/2–2 ½ in across, with six scoop-shaped sepals of a delicate pale pink with darker reverse forming a saucer-shaped flower. The foliage, like that of all armandiis, is a striking bronze colour. 'Snowdrift' is pure white, with a flat flower up to 8cm/3in across comprised of six flat, overlapping sepals with pointed tips. These varieties are not always offered for sale at local garden centres but are well worth seeking out from good clematis specialists.

Clematis armandii should be given a sunny, sheltered position, with plenty of space to develop fully. In an ideal spot, it will make up to 9m/30ft of growth, although it will usually stand hard pruning immediately the flowers have faded, if necessary. *DL*

3/4/97 - All Watered. Cabbage shoots.

5/4/97 - Big Parafin Heater On.

6/4/97 - Build New Shelves. Tom. Plants in Grow Bags.
All Watered. Plant Potatoes.
3 Rows Sharps Express + 3 small side G'House.
4 Rows Kerrs Pinks (closest to Fence.)
Cucumber into bigger Pot.
Carrot Seedling come up. Brussel Sprouts shoots.
New Front Fence to go up.
Sowed Lettuce (Unwins Lollo Rossa) ¼ Pkt (in Modules
Heater On.

7/4/97 Sowed Oregano + Chilli Peppers.
Pricked out Cabbages. 2 small shelves up.
Rocket starting to show in Rows outside.
3 Tom. Plant Seeds shoots showing.

8/4/97 - Beetroot Shoots up. ± 6 Tom. Plant (seeds) Shoots
A Few Carrot shoots showing.

14/4/97 - Pricked out Carrots. Feed Plants All.

15/4/97 - Filled Butt with Hose water. Watered Garden.

17/4/97 - Nearly All Sweetcorn. 1 Chilli shoots small
Put out All Green lettuce + Flowers to
adjust to outdoors. Peas all coming
through. Oregano coming through. a few
Blackcurrant bush. showing beginnings
of fruit, Rasps. bush taken well. Garlic
thickening up stems.

22/4/97. Lettuces now
outdoors, two plots next
to greenhouse. Weather
very dry, two frosts
this week. Thought i'd
lost the lettuces but they
survived. Fed them to
recover. Mary got
Rody bush from Fiona
and put next to Balloon
and Balloney. Gas
BBQ in corner of
garden. Slabs from
garden to go in greenhouse
Nipped buds off tomatoes

ORGANIC MULCHES

To conserve water and prevent weeds,
bulky organic mulches should be at
least 5cm/2in thick. While this is not
usually a problem, a few shallow-
rooted plants such as members of the
rhododendron family, can be damaged
if their roots are buried too deeply.

Thick mulches, especially semi-
permanent ones like chipped wood
and gravel, also make it difficult for
planting through once they are spread.

In addition, frequent, regular
mulching raises the height of borders,
often meaning that the mulch, assisted
by birds, spills on to adjacent
lawns and paths.

Strawberries 5 (mid season) 5 late
bayh £6.50 mb to front plot.
25/04/97. May fed all plants in
greenhouse + strawbs. Sunny
day up to 80° in greenhouse.

SOAPBOX

CHOOSING A MULCH

Spreading a mulch on top of the soil when it is warm and moist will help to conserve that moisture, prevent weed growth and keep roots cool in hot, dry summer weather.

Originally, mulches were mainly farmyard and stable manure, spent hops and well-rotted compost, though with increasing urbanization and smaller gardens, substitutes such as peat began to appear. More recent materials include commercially composted bark, bark and wood chips, coir, cocoa shell, home-shredded garden waste, mushroom compost, black polythene and semi-permeable sheeting, gravel and stone chippings. There are also some bizarre recommendations around for re-using domestic refuse such as old carpet and underlay.

No one mulching material is perfect in every way. Weeds can be introduced into the garden in farmyard manure if not well enough rotted, and if garden compost has not been correctly made, seeds can remain to germinate in the wrong places. Leaving aside the environmental arguments against using peat, a dried-out peat mulch can form a waterproof thatch actually preventing rainwater from reaching the soil. Composted bark is expensive, and, as it is not fully rotted, can rob the soil of nitrates as it breaks down. The latter also applies to wood chippings and shredded waste; furthermore, as these are rarely sterilized, there is a chance of introducing or spreading disease around the garden. Cocoa shell is light so easily blows off the borders; it also makes the soil increasingly acid as it rots. Conversely, mushroom compost is alkaline, and regular use can raise soil pH to a harmful degree. (Take the pH of your garden soil into account before choosing either of these options.) Polythene and other sheeting looks unsightly unless disguised with bark chippings or gravel. And old carpet and similar materials simply look appalling unless similarly camouflaged, which cancels out much of the money-saving advantage of recycling such waste material. *DL*

30/4/97 — Peas up couple of inches. Previous 3
days - A-thinned out Rocket, weeded all. Watered.
Sage planted out Rockery, Parsley, Dill.

8/5/97 - Fed Plants, Door open during day.
4 Days of rain. Butt Full

Friday 9 in May,
Planted out Cauliflowers + carrots.
Cabbage + Brussels, +Beetroot treated +Nigella rosa.
with Root Powder first,
Earthed up Potatoe chits
appearing. Treated with Incectide.
Slug pellets down.

Saturday, 10 in May.
String up for Tomato Plants.
Potatoes through.
Sat, 17 in May
Sticks for Peas.
Planted Bush Peas in
centre of rows + rest
of carrots, Bush Rosemary
Dill, Oregeno, Basil (some
left in tray).
Fertilized + well watered
+ Fed.
Sunday. Peas reaching
towards sticks.
Changed Rows of Potatoes

Sowing seeds in divided tray

PLANNING SUMMER BEDDING

WHENEVER POSSIBLE, I start sowing my bedding plants in January, but there are times when circumstances prevent me from doing this and the task has to be delayed. Granted, some of them don't make as bushy a plant and others flower later, but they still give a decent show and fill the garden with colour in summer. I'm fortunate in that I have a heated greenhouse and heated propagators, but if you haven't got these facilities, don't worry – just sow seed later, in March and April, when days are lighter and warmer.

Start off with antirrhinums, salvias, lobelia, begonias, pansies, violas, zonal pelargoniums (geraniums), *Laurentia axillaris* and sweet peas. These are quickly followed by petunias, verbena, impatiens, gazanias, French and African marigolds, tagetes, ageratum, stocks, *Phlox drummondii*, mesembryanthemum and alyssum. The last ones to go in are asters, dahlias and zinnias, because these are quick to germinate, fast-growing, quite tender and don't like a chill.

The hardy annuals are best sown directly into the beds where they are to flower and to get a good show in summer they need to go in during April. However, in the colder parts of the country the ground isn't always workable at this time of the year. You can get over this by sowing the seeds in divided trays then, or do so a week or two earlier in a cold greenhouse, cold frame or placed end-to-end under a line of cloches. Using the trays enables you to plant out later with very little root disturbance, which hardy annuals resent, when ground conditions have improved, at the end of April or the beginning of May. *FD*

NOTES

_____

_____

_____

_____

_____

_____

_____

_____

_____

_____

_____

_____

_____

GARDENER'S TIP

*M*op-head and lace-cap hydrangeas flower on wood produced during the previous season, so any stems that bloomed last year should be cut back almost down to the ground, but only take the branches of *Hydrangea paniculata* down to two buds from the base, just as we treat *Buddleia davidii*.

The only way to get winter colour from the bark of *Cornus alba* (dogwood) or *Salix alba* (willow) is to cut them back to about 20cm/8in above soil level in spring.

Pruning buddleia

SHRUBS TO PRUNE IN SPRING

DECIDUOUS SHRUBS THAT give us colour and interest on the current year's growth by either flowering or producing decorative bark in summer, autumn or winter should be pruned in spring. The precise timing of this operation depends on the weather and location. Usually the end of February or early March are appropriate times, but the moment can vary from one year to another and from county to county. You'll know it's time to get on with the job when the buds start to break and new shoots appear.

Try to finish pruning bush and climbing roses by mid March, although some gardeners prefer to cut them back in the autumn or during the winter. However, the late-flowering hybrid clematis such as Jackmanii are always best pruned in spring, down to 20–25cm/8–10in from the base.

Hardy fuchsias can be chopped off a few centimetres above soil level. The new basal shoots will be stronger and more floriferous than if they were only cut half back. *FD*

CUTTINGS FOR CONTAINERS

Container plants are justifiably very popular for they add colour to parts of the garden that would otherwise be dull, such as patios, window ledges and walls when they are grown in tubs, windowboxes and hanging baskets. Even if you don't have a garden or only have a backyard, you can enjoy growing plants this way; they not only give you colour during the summer, but by choosing carefully you will also have a show in winter.

Many of the plants used in containers can be raised from seed, but others must be grown from cuttings. Pelargoniums (geraniums) are typical examples, as dozens of varieties are available as seed, but if you want variegated foliage, double flowers or the more floriferous, trailing, ivy-leaved types which are ideal for containers, you must raise them from cuttings.

Cascading fuchsias look marvellous in hanging baskets, while the more upright-growing types are ideal centre plants in patio tubs. If you want a specific colour to blend in with the rest of your planting, the only way to ensure this is to take cuttings. The same applies to the light blue *Lobelia richardii* and the lilac, double form 'Kathleen Mallard', trailing verbena and bidens, the variegated trailing nepeta, *Helichrysum petiolatum* and, of course, the small leaved ivies.

Granted, you have to overwinter these plants in a frost-free place, but then all you need to do to increase your stock is root the tips of young shoots in a gritty compost at a temperature of 16°C/60°F. Once rooted, pot them up individually into 8cm/3in pots filled with potting compost and, when they are large enough, harden them off and plant them. *FD*

Pelargonium shoot as cut
from the plant

Trim the shoot below a node and
remove the lower leaves

Insert the cutting in a soil-based
seedling compost and it should
root within a couple of weeks

NOTES

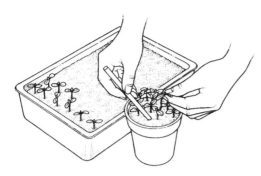

SEEDLING SENSE

Mᴏsᴛ ᴏf ᴍʏ bedding plants are sown in 9cm/3½ in pots, because I grow so many different varieties and this method enables me to pack a great many in the heated propagators at one time. If you are only growing a few of course, you could use seed trays.

I get the best results by mixing equal quantities of John Innes seed compost and a soil-less type, adding a little vermiculite to create a more open mixture and retain moisture.

The pots are filled, tamped down gently, stood in water until the compost is soaked right through and then topped off with 3mm/⅛ in of vermiculite, which is also tamped. The seed is scattered thinly on top of this and then the pots are topped off with another thin layer of vermiculite and pressed down again. Very fine seeds such as lobelias, begonias and petunias are not covered; these are left on the surface, watered with a very fine spray and placed in the heated propagator at the required temperature for germination.

When the seedlings are 3mm/⅛ in high the pots are transferred to the cold propagator in the heated greenhouse where the temperature is 10°C/50°F. A week later they go on to the open bench, where they stay until they are large enough to be pricked out. I set them 5cm/2in apart into seed trays, or allot one to each compartment of a divided tray, using a mixture of John Innes No.1 potting compost, a soil-less compost and vermiculite. I choose the strongest seedlings of self-coloured varieties, but when pricking out mixtures, I select differing leaf and stem colours and various heights. *FD*

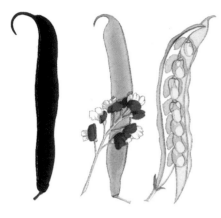

A BROADER BEANFEAST

To most people, beanz meanz . . . traditional runners, French or broad beans. But delve into the seed catalogues and you'll find a gourmets' delight. Try edible antiques such as 'Green Windsor' broad bean (known since 1809) and 'Golden Butter' French bean (1882), which were bred for flavour rather than enormous yields. 'Painted Lady' runner bean (1855) is best known for her bi-coloured pink and white flowers, making this a productive and pretty climber to cover a fence. Or go for modern stringless runners ('Lady Di') and pencil-thin filet varieties of French bean ('Aramis'). Purple-podded beans like 'Purple Tepee' look pretty enough to include in a flower bed, and are easy to spot when picking – the purple colour disappears during cooking.

Where space is short, go for climbing varieties of both runner and French bean – you get more from the space then with dwarf kinds, though the latter are more likely to succeed in a windy site. For specially large crops go for giant runners like 'Enorma'; a show variety that also makes excellent eating. Or if you have plenty of space, try growing kidney and haricot beans for drying – most varieties can also be picked young, shelled, and used fresh in much the same way as peas. Both dwarf and climbing varieties are available. The pea bean (whose seeds are round and prettily patterned in maroon and white) and the old Italian 'Marvel of Venice' are absolutely delicious dual-purpose varieties, found in specialist catalogues. You can even grow flageolets – pale green elongated haricot beans for use fresh or dried – and soya beans, though both need a long hot summer to produce a crop fit to dry. *SP*

NOTES

Cosmos atrosanguineus
PLANT PORTRAIT

*P*icture a bushy 60cm / 2ft tall mini-dahlia with small, chocolate-scented double 'black' flowers from June to November, and you almost have *Cosmos atrosanguineus* – the conservation success of the nineties. Seed of *Cosmos atrosanguineus*, a native of Mexico, was first brought to this country in 1835. The plant became a favourite in Victorian gardens, but declined dangerously when changing garden fashions ousted flowers in favour of easy-care lawns and shrubs. Chocolate cosmos was rescued from the brink of extinction comparatively recently. Nurseries propagated it rapidly, and though at first scarce and pricy, it was soon the 'must-have' plant for fashionable gardens.

Despite its near miss with oblivion, *Cosmos atrosanguineus* is surprisingly easy to propagate. Take basal cuttings from the new growth in early summer. (Plants come into growth much later than dahlias.) These root in time for a small tuber to form, which allows the dormant plant to survive the winter – late cuttings fail. I always grow my plants in pots plunged to their rims in the ground during summer, then lift and store complete with surrounding soil (prevented from getting dust dry), in a frost-free shed or greenhouse for the winter. *SP*

THE SLUG QUESTION

THERE CAN'T REALLY be any doubt in the matter. The number-one pest for most gardeners is slimy, one-footed, variously coloured but voraciously hungry: the slug, of course. Yes, despite their relatively lowly place in the evolutionary scheme of things, vegetarian garden molluscs spell trouble.

The slug problem can be combated in four ways, although I don't pretend that any really spell total control. First, avoidance; clearly the most attractive option. You could try not growing the soft-foliaged plants that appeal so much to slugs – not easy, of course, when the list inevitably includes such important plants as lettuces. Or perhaps you could grow your plants somewhere that the slugs find hard to reach: hostas in pots offer an excellent example. Or maybe you could trying growing certain plants at a time of year when slugs are less active. The early potato crop, for instance, often escapes damage from subterranean slugs, which only really get into their stride when the main crop is maturing.

The second option is to protect your plants with a physical barrier across which they are loathe to drag their slimy bodies. Powdery materials such as ash from the grate are ideal, although they need renewing regularly after rain. Alternatively, minutely spiny twigs such as gorse will act as a very effective deterrent, although there is clearly a limit to the number of plants that can be protected in this way (and the prickles can put off gardeners as well as slugs).

The third option is a baited trap which is inspected regularly and the contents disposed of. Upturned grapefruit or orange skins are the simplest; sunken jars containing beer rather more sophisticated, as the inmates are likely to have drowned before you reach them.

Finally, there is direct control. Traditional chemicals such as metaldehyde in pellet, liquid or tape form are undeniably effective but unless concealed under slates, may attract pets and wild life. (You also need to clear away the bodies before they enter the food chain.) Which leaves the latest option: biological control using a culture of specially grown nematodes (eelworms). The technique is effective, given the right conditions of warm, moist soil but, like everything else, it will still leave plenty of slugs for next year. *SB*

NOTES

T O O L B O X

U S E F U L   G A D G E T S   F O R   S P R I N G

MEASURING STICK

Unlike the flowers, my vegetables are all grown in straight rows. To achieve this military precision when I set out my seeds and young plants in spring, the gadget I find most useful is my measuring stick, which was handed down to me many years ago. It's just a 1.5m/5ft length of broom handle which is painted green and marked every 7.5cm/3in alternately with black and red, so it makes spacing out plants very simple. I use it to measure the distances between rows in the beds and then the plants in the rows. The result all looks very neat and makes weeding and other cultivations much easier. FD

BORDER SPADE

My border spade has been my trusty friend since I was ten years old. It is so well used that its blade is as polished as stainless steel and as sharp as a razor. It is much less tiring to work with than a digging spade; consequently, although it is smaller, I get much more work done with it in the same period. It's just the job for a quick turning over of the vegetable plot before spring sowings. And the knife-sharp blade makes a wonderful edging iron for the rest of the summer. DL

SWAN-NECKED DRAW HOE

I've spent much of my gardening life looking for the perfect hoe, which is why I now have a shedful. My favourite for hoeing in confined spaces is a slightly unusual draw hoe resembling a long-handled onion hoe. It has a small half-moon-shaped head and a swan neck. It's light, elegant and very precise – almost like a surgical instrument, great for going between rows of veg, or hooking out bigger weeds. SP

Measuring stick

Border spade

Swan-necked draw hoe

BETTER HANGING BASKETS

A hanging basket burgeoning with health adds the perfect finishing touch to a fine summer display. A well-cared-for basket can last for five months; getting things right early on in the season will help it to give of its best throughout this time.

Don't be in too much of a hurry to put out your summer baskets. There could still be some really cold, windy weather in May, which would play havoc with tender young plants. If possible, plant up your baskets in the greenhouse and allow them to grow on under glass for around four weeks. The plants will then be established and the baskets well furnished when they are hung up in their final positions. If no greenhouse is available, leave planting for a few weeks, and then let the plants settle down for a while in a sheltered place at ground level outdoors before hanging them up; they will soon catch up with the warmer weather.

The most effective baskets are still those with wire sides lined with moss or moss substitute. The eventual effect you are looking for is a basket completely covered with plants, with no wire or moss showing. Although plants growing on the top will eventually hang down and cover the sides, introduce some through the basket sides as planting progresses. Use an old toilet roll holder to protect the roots as you push them through and space them so the ones nearer the top won't smother those lower down.

Special hanging-basket composts containing water-retaining substances and wetting agents are available, but any good potting compost will do – mixing in a teaspoonful per basket of water-retaining polymer granules will help to keep it damp, though this is not an excuse for lazy watering! The compost should be kept nicely moist throughout the season; this may mean watering several times a day in very hot weather. If you have several baskets, it may be worthwhile considering a simple automatic system – these are readily available and easy to install.

To keep a basket growing and flowering well for a long period it must be fed. The compost will contain enough fertilizer to get the basket started, then a liquid feed should be given regularly according to the manufacturers' instructions. Otherwise, add a slow-release fertilizer to the compost at planting time.

With these simple guidelines for success, your baskets should delight you all summer long. *DL*

DESIGNER POTATOES

POTATOES, ONCE BLAMED for burgeoning waistlines, are today the rising stars of the healthy-eating campaign; rich in fibre, unrefined carbohydrates and vitamin C, and, unless you eat them dripping in melted butter, low in fat. So dig in. But don't take up valuable space growing what you could buy in the shops. Go for something special. Those first new potatoes of the season (far tastier than Egyptian imports), and some of the 'rare' spuds only available as 'seed' from specialist suppliers, pitch the humble spud firmly into the gourmet league.

For the earliest earlies, plant a few sprouted tubers of a forcing variety such as 'Dunluce' singly in large pots, or six per growing bag, and keep in a frost-free greenhouse till May, when they can be moved outdoors to make room for other crops. For growing outdoors, one of the best earlies is 'Rocket'.

To follow, some of the tastiest 'tatties' around are antique varieties – 'British Queen' (floury second early), 'Ratte' (yellow-fleshed waxy second early), 'Up-To-Date' and 'Pink Fir Apple' (both waxy-textured late main-croppers). Modern varieties, however, give heavier yields: 'Heather', 'Sante' and 'Kestrel' are good-looking, tasty and productive. For eating cold, try 'Linzer Delikatess', though 'Ratte' and 'Pink Fir Apple' make superb salad spuds, too. *SP*

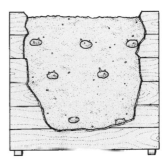

VERTICAL POTATOES

Short of space? Then grow your
spuds vertically instead of
horizontally. Special potato tubs are
available, but a compost bin filled
with a mixture of well-rotted
compost and topsoil and planted with
three 'layers' of six seed potatoes
separated by a 15cm/6in depth of soil
gives a huge crop from a small space.
Feed and water well during the
season, and you can start rummaging
for the odd spud well before lifting
time. Black gold!

MOISTURE-LOVING PLANTS

Damp spots need not be a problem – it's merely a question of picking your plants. Marginal plants are a good bet for ground that never dries out, as well as pondsides – *Iris laevigata* and *I. ensata*, *Lobelia syphilitica*, aruncus (goat's beard), carex (sedges) and corkscrew rush are all at home here. The striking skunk cabbage (*Lysichiton*) with its huge yellow or white spathes and distinctive odour, is rather an acquired taste for many gardens. For a more cultivated look in moist borders, try feathery lythrum, cimicifuga, filipendula and astilbe flowers with the solid reddish rhubarb-like leaves of rheum; or fragile Japanese lemon-and-lime striped grass *Hakonechloa macra* 'Aureola' with huge hostas.

A favourite group at the end of my garden contains heart shaped tri-coloured houttuynia leaves and dramatic *Peltiphyllum peltatum* leaves like saucers-on-sticks, with spikes of coppery *Schizostylis coccinea* for the end of the season. If a 'statement' is needed (and space is no problem), you can be bold with giant gunnera, a bed of rodgersia or huge clump of hardy arum lily (*Zantedeschia aethiopica* 'Crowborough') – all have great architectural value. Or make a 'cameo' of moisture-loving shrubs. For a wild garden, how about miscanthus (ornamental sugar cane), *Viburnum opulus* and ornamental elders (*Sambucus nigra* cultivars – 'Guincho Purple' is specially pretty with deep purple leaves and palest pink flowers). Species roses appreciate moist, heavy soil – rugosa types are among the most tolerant. On heath-like damp acid soil, birches, cowberry (*Vaccinum vitis-idaea*) and bog myrtle (*Myrica gale*) thrive in each others' company.

Though most moisture-loving plants need a reasonably sunny aspect, there is always the odd corner in shade to tackle. Make the most of this 'problem' spot to grow sophisticated ferns, cultivated celandines and arching stems of Solomon's seal with stunning summer-flowering toad lilies (*Tricyrtis*) – truly a series of classic combinations. *SP*

NOTES

D R A W I N G   B O A R D

M A K I N G   A   S H A D Y   A R B O U R

A N ARBOUR, in simple terms, is a sitting place. It usually consists of a framework over which attractive climbing plants are grown to form a shady retreat, preferably with an attractive view. The arbours of great, historic gardens were often elaborate affairs, but there is no need to go to these lengths to construct something which is both functional and pleasing to the eye.

Ready-made arbours and gazebos are widely available, but it is very satisfying to design your own, using sawn hardwood or softwood or rustic poles, with stout supports for the framework and fencing-quality trellis as infill panels. Metal post supports will prevent premature rotting of the base of the vertical supports. Treat the structure with a 'plant-friendly' preservative before planting up. Wrought iron or other metal is a good alternative to wood.

It is advisable to pave the area within the arbour; once it becomes covered with plants, it will be too shady to grow grass. *DL*

Suitable plants for an arbour (F = fragrant):
Large-flowered hybrid clematis,
e.g. 'Gypsy Queen'
Clematis flammula (F) for large arbours only
Climbing rose 'Etoile de Holland'
Eccremocarpus scaber
Jasminum x stephanense (F)
Lonicera periclymenum 'Graham Thomas' (F)
Trachelospermum jasminoides (F) for
warm areas only
Vitis purpurea for large arbours only

CHOICE CONTAINER

STONE TROUGH

A T THIS TIME of the year the most admired container in my garden is an old natural stone trough planted up mainly with alpines to resemble a miniature landscape. It was given to me by a farmer friend who lives nearby and I was delighted, as I knew it would match the stonework of the cottage; in fact they both probably came from the same local quarry.

The first thing I did was to put crocks over the holes in the bottom, then I added a 5cm/2in layer of large gravel, before filling it with a very gritty compost. I found an old, gnarled piece of oak while I was out walking, so I half buried this diagonally across the trough and planted round it.

There's a small specimen of *Juniperus communis* 'Compressa' to add height towards one corner. *Cotoneaster congestus* 'Nanus' hangs over the front edge; this is covered with green leaves all year, and produces white flowers in summer and glossy, red berries in autumn – which stay on until the birds decide to take them. I've planted a couple of saxifrages in it, *Saxifraga* 'Gregor Mendel', which has small, primrose-yellow flowers and the deeper coloured *Saxifragra* 'Gold Dust', which make a bright splash in early spring. In one corner, just covering the stone edge, is *Sempervivum arachnoideum* with its small rosettes, covered with what look like spiders' webs, and *Sempervivum* 'Jubilee', which has green and red foliage. I've also planted one of my favourite *Dianthus* in it, 'Little Jock', which has greyish leaves and tiny pink flowers during the summer. *FD*

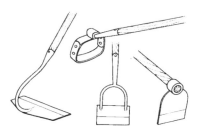

SPRING TIDY-UP

ONE YEAR'S SEEDING means seven years' weeding: the old gardeners' saying is quite right, too. In neglected gardens, any cultivation brings buried seeds to the surface where, exposed to light, they germinate. But even without setting seed, some weeds spread like wildfire – notably perennial nasties with running roots such as couch grass, bindweed, ground elder and horsetail. The only remedy is to get ahead of the game at the start of the gardening year, using either chemical or physical remedies.

Chemicals are not all as black as they are tarnished; they may be the only way for some people to cope with problem gardens. Glyphosate-based weedkillers are very useful for clearing vacant ground of both annual and perennial weeds – once treated, weeds die and the ground can safely be replanted. Such products can also be painted or sprayed on to individual weeds growing between cultivated plants, so long as you take care not to spray any on to plants you don't want to kill. Regular treatment will eradicate even difficult problem weeds. Casoron G4 is less well known, but useful for keeping mature tree and shrub borders weed-free; however, it can't be used where there are flowers or bulbs.

Of the 'greener' physical remedies, mulching is the first line of defence. A 5cm/2in thick layer of well-rotted organic matter spread round shrubs and perennials every spring helps smother out germinating weed seedlings. Hoeing is the second defence. Soil with a high organic content is easy to hoe, as it stays soft and moist – so mulching helps, even if the odd seedling does come up in the mulch later. To work well, hoeing needs doing regularly. I find a weekly run-round with a favourite hoe keeps me on top of weeds before they grow big enough to slow things down. Alternatively, perforated black plastic can be spread over soil for a permanently weed-free finish; in ornamental beds, hide it under a layer of chipped bark or gravel – a finish that sets off plants to a T. *SP*

GOOD COMPANIONS

BULBS AND WOODLAND PLANTS BENEATH SHRUBS

The mini-woodland environment towards the edge of a shrubbery can be brought to life with a variety of bulbs and other plants adapted to thrive in cool conditions of dappled shade and a leaf-mould-rich soil.

One cannot fail to be delighted by drifts of the choicest form of winter aconite, *Eranthis* 'Cilicica' with bronzy foliage and deep gold flowers, the starry white windflower, *Anemone nemorosa*, or the true English bluebell, *Hyacinthoides non-scripta*, while snowdrops are equally as happy in such a position as they are naturalized in grass. Hardy cyclamen will soon spread once established, and will delight with their dainty blooms from September through February, when the m a r b l e d - l e a v e d *Cyclamen hederifolium* and fragrant *Cyclamen cilicium* are succeeded by crimson, pink and white *Cyclamen coum*. These can be followed by the beautiful erythroniums, the dog's tooth violets, which are somewhat exacting in their requirements of moist, well-drained, humus-rich, lime-free soil, but are well worth persevering with, from the dainty, violet, pink and white *Erythronium dens-canis* to the exotic yellow 'Pagoda' and outstanding *E. revolutum* 'White Beauty'.

This is also an area to grow such choice herbaceous plants as that charming relative of the primula, *Dodecatheon* (sometimes known as the shooting star); the lovely Japanese painted fern, *Athyrium n i p p o n i c u m* 'Pictum'; the purple form of wood spurge, *E u p h o r b i a a m y g d a l o i d e s* 'Rubra'; the curious *Asarum europaeum* or wild ginger, with its shiny, leathery, leafy discs and the Lenten rose, *Helleborus orientalis*. And easily grown favourites, so evocative of the shady cottage garden, like foxgloves and sweet violets, should never be forgotten. *DL*

NOTES

SPRING CHECKLIST

❦ When herbaceous perennials have grown too large or are getting old and are no longer floriferous, lift them in early spring, divide and replant the outer, young, healthy growths.

❦ If Hybrid Tea, Floribunda and climbing roses are to follow well all summer, complete pruning by the end of March, and follow this with a feed and a thick mulch.

❦ While the ground is cool, but still workable, sowings of broad beans, round-seeded peas and parsnips can be made if you are to have the benefit of early crops.

❦ Before tomatoes, cucumbers and so on are planted in the cold greenhouse at the end of April/beginning of May, be sure to clean it thoroughly both inside and out.

❦ Autumn and winter brassicas need a long season of growth if they are to produce a good crop. Sow them in early April in a cold frame or under a cloche.

❦ The least expensive way to make a lawn is to sow grass seed in spring. There are plenty of mixtures to choose from, depending on where they are to be sown and the purpose of the lawn.

❦ To get a heavy yield from maincrop potatoes, plant them by mid-April, in ground that has been dug deeply and had plenty of well-rotted manure incorporated into it.

❦ When spring bedding has finished at the beginning of May, clear the beds immediately. Prepare them for the summer show by digging them over and applying a high-potash base fertilizer.

❦ Runner, climbing and dwarf French beans go in at the beginning of May, sown directly into the ground where they are to crop. Covering them with fleece will help them to germinate and protect them from any late frosts.

❦ When planting up the borders with bedding plants, start with the hardiest ones such as antirrhinums and pansies, leaving the more tender ones until last, but do make sure that they have all been hardened off beforehand. *FD*

Summer

W E WAIT FOR IT, and wait for it; but it is always too brief by far. So often in recent years, I have had to sympathize with Lord Byron, who offered the profound observation that the English winter ends in July, to recommence in August. But this year, it will be different – be assured that I predicted the last mild winter with great accuracy, so my track record is sound. To me, summer is a time for enjoying the garden, for savouring the results of your labours. In either new garden or old, summer is not a time for horticultural haste. I know of course that modern container-production of shrubs, trees and herbaceous perennials means that it is perfectly possible to plant them at almost any season of the year with only a modicum of disturbance to their roots. But why hurry? In an established garden, you can wait until the more appropriate conditions of autumn; in a new one, you will have had no time to prepare the soil.

Although I commend garden enjoyment, I hope that your entire summer will not be spent in reclining in deck chair or bowed over barbecue. There are routine tasks to attend to and top of everyone's list must be the inevitable lawn mowing. I cannot for the life of me understand why so many people complain about it. I positively enjoy the task and I can put the world to rights during the couple of hours it takes me to complete the rounds. I suppose if I am truly honest, it is the end result that pleases me even more, and I am conservative enough to appreciate a carefully striped lawn such as only a cylinder mower can achieve. In practice, I don't bring out the cylinder mower until May, preferring to let the big rotary deal with the roughness that is winter's legacy at the start of the season. I never apply fertilizer to the lawn in the height of summer; provided an early-season dressing has been applied, drenching costly liquid feed on to the grass during the summer is really a short-lived cosmetic treatment that doesn't repay the time and expense. *SB*

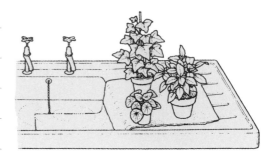

HOUSEPLANTS ON HOLIDAY

AS YOU PACK for this summer's foreign trip, spare a thought for those long-suffering members of the family left at home – houseplants. How will they cope without you? Although 'horti-kennels' can occasionally be found, most of us have to make other arrangements.

Top of the list is the kind neighbour. For the price of a return favour when they next go away, your plants are assured the five-star treatment – provided they are plantspeople themselves.

Plan B is the DIY self-watering kit. This involves laying a damp towel on the kitchen drainer, standing well-watered plants on top, and dangling the spare end into a sink-full of water to act as a wick. This will keep a dozen plants fresh for a fortnight. A similar system can be set up in the bathroom, with the damp towel laid in the bottom of the bath, and a container of water standing on the end of it – ideal for taller specimen plants or a bigger collection – but it is vital to avoid using cleaning products or bleach just beforehand, as the fumes are unfriendly to plants. Test-run the system a few weeks before H-day so you have time for fine-tuning if need be.

Alternatively, put plants outdoors and let Mother Nature care for them. In practice she needs a hand, so plunge pots to their rim in damp soil in the shade under trees, 'mulch' with moist cocoa-shell (which also deters slugs) and give them a good soaking just before you leave. Even if there is no rain while you are away, this should last a fortnight. (Don't cover plants with crop-protection 'fleece' or cloches – they'll get far too hot.)

Given proper planning, you may be amazed to find on your return that the plants have benefited as much from their summer holiday as you have! *SP*

FLOWERS IN YOUR LAWN

Flowery meads were vital ingredients of medieval gardens and, after a long period with lawns like green velvet, they are now making a come-back. How do we achieve a flowery lawn? Left to its own devices (that is, thoroughly neglected) any lawn will start sprouting 'wildflowers' of the undesirable kind. But it is surprisingly difficult to turn a suburban lawn into a decent flowering meadow. Simply sprinkling packets of wildflower seed over the top doesn't work. The trick is to buy or raise good plants, and actually set them into the lawn – then they'll spread naturally. (Choose grassland species such as field poppy or corn cockle or, for dappled shade, woodland flowers like greater stitchwort and primrose.)

If you are starting a flowering lawn from scratch, mix 500g/1lb grass with a packet of wildflower seed and sow in the usual way, at 30–60g/1–2oz per square metre or yard, without any fertilizer. (A special grass seed mixture is available for shady areas.)

Establishing a flowering lawn is one thing; taking care of it is quite different from 'polite', well-groomed turf. A flowering lawn must be left long to flower and set seed – vital for perpetuating the species. (The only wildflowers that stand close cutting are violets and speedwell.) So a cut in early spring, followed by another after the last flowers have shed their seed, in late summer or early autumn depending on the species used, is all it needs.

Never use feed or weedkiller. Their rather unkempt appearance means flowering lawns are usually confined to a wildlife area at the end of the garden, along with native trees and shrubs. Use one or two kinds of flower distributed evenly throughout for a meadowy look, or for a more natural effect, dot different groups about randomly. Or combine a flowering lawn with a normal one by 'contour mowing' – leaving flowery boundaries uncut, with an informal shaped close-cropped area near the house. It looks lovely! *SP*

Clean bulbs and store them in a cool, dark place

TULIP TACTICS

THE LARGE-HEADED hybrid tulips are among the most striking of our formal spring bedding flowers, yet they can cause disappointment. Whereas many other spring bulbs once planted can be forgotten for years and will reward with an increasingly spectacular display, tulips can let you down, especially after the first season.

Tulips are natives of warmer climates than that of the United Kingdom; they come from southern Europe, west and central Asia and north Africa, and, although hardy in Britain, survive best in warm, well-drained conditions, where, after flowering, the bulb can ripen properly for the following season. They will not tolerate long periods of frozen soil, especially once the flower bud has started to emerge.

The usual reason for failure is that bulbs were planted too early and not deeply enough in the autumn, started to grow almost immediately, so that the new shoots and flower buds were subsequently damaged by a long period of penetrating frost. Even if the first year's flowering is successful, many people find that few, if any, flowers are produced the following year – also due to premature growth in the autumn, followed by frost damage, and often made worse by a cold, wet summer or unsuitable growing conditions.

For this reason, it is often thought best to lift the bulbs once the foliage has died down completely, clean them and store them in a cool, dry, dark place until November, when they can be replanted safely without any fear of premature growth. In fact I have managed to keep several clumps growing from year to year without lifting by planting them somewhat deeper than normal, with about 15–18cm/6–7in of soil above the 'nose' of the bulb, which reduces the effect on them of extreme weather conditions.

However, because garden hybrid tulips are such architectural flowers, they are perhaps best displayed in formal bedding schemes rather than naturalized like daffodils, and so should be lifted and stored until late autumn as a matter of course when the summer bedding is planted. Exceptions are the 'botanical' (wild) forms, which naturalize successfully in a rock-garden setting. *DL*

*N*eed a low-maintenance garden? A Tudor-style knot garden is the answer – no need for a mower or any tools. Just a rake for the coloured gravel paths, and a hedge trimmer to keep the miniature box hedge pattern in trim thrice yearly. Modern featureless gardens? Gadzooks! Not on your Nell Gwynn!

S O A P B O X

IN FAVOUR OF ECCENTRICITY

What has happened to the great British tradition of gardening eccentricity? Modern developments are fine; today, anyone can have their own designer garden, hanging baskets or patio. But much of the individuality has vanished. Who, nowadays, installs topiary chessmen and steam trains, fallen gothic arches, or a cave for the resident hermit? Yet I think some early garden eccentricities would be surprisingly at home in the modern garden.

Take the medieval stew pond for instance; fish suppers on tap – an ideal recession-beater. (A deer park is even better and has the advantage of keeping the grass down.) Or decorative fruit trees. In France, the Emperor Napoleon's name was trained in trees, and in Victorian England, entire crowns, gazebos and decorative screens were once formed in fruit. (Imagine the name of your house – 'Dun-prunin' – growing in the front garden?) And add vintage Great Garden Jokes – jets of water erupting up through paving slabs or garden seats – to take visitors by surprise.

If space is short, how about a mount – a junior hill as seen in all the best gardens of Henry VIII's day? With a planted path spiralling up to the top, it gives you a far longer walk round the garden then you'd have on the flat. It also lets you view your neighbours' gardens advantageously from above. *SP*

PREVENTATIVE MEASURES FOR PESTS AND DISEASES

IT APPLIES TO garden health as much as anything else in life: 'prevention is better than cure'. When you acquire transplant-sized herbaceous perennials, crowns, rootstocks or young trees and shrubs, always inspect them carefully. Whenever possible, choose perfect-quality plants; otherwise cut away any obviously damaged or diseased parts.

Some diseases can be carried on seeds. Dusting onion seed with a systemic fungicide will all but eliminate one of the most important of them, neck rot. And if you save seed or take cuttings from your own plants, it is most important that you do so only from those individuals that are themselves healthy and vigorous.

Perhaps the commonest source of problems among planting stock lies with bulbs of ornamentals. Here, the best suppliers take great trouble to raise and sell only high-quality, healthy material, but inferior job lots are regrettably still to be found. Planting these in your garden may result in poor plants with few or small flowers; but more importantly, it may introduce into your garden some problem not there already. And don't forget that many diseases, once established in the soil, will stay there for a very long time.

And finally, remember that a tidy garden is generally a healthy garden. Given that pests do require hiding places, and given that many disease-causing fungi have the annoying ability to survive on plant remains, from thence to attack our growing crops, the clearing away of garden rubbish is essential. The pile of pots or old seed trays behind the greenhouse will provide just the conditions beneath which slugs will hide during the daytime. And the mound of rotten pea sticks left for several years in the corner of the vegetable plot is an irresistible temptation to coral-spot disease and to woodlice. *SB*

GARDENER'S TIP

It is particularly important only to buy new stock
of virus-susceptible plants
from reputable suppliers
and, in many instances
(fruit trees and bushes and
potatoes, most notably),
only to buy those that are
certified in some manner
as virus-free. Remember,
moreover, that once such
potatoes, strawberries or
other virus-free stocks are
planted in your garden,
they will inevitably become
contaminated as aphids and
other agents introduce
virus into them. It is false
economy to save from the
stock for propagation,
therefore; buy fresh each
time you plant.

NOTES

GARDENER'S TIP

*P*revent trees and tall-
growing shrubs from being
rocked in the ground or
broken off in the wind by
securing them to a stout
post of treated timber.

STAKING AND SUPPORTS

Many of the plants we grow need supporting, and by many, I mean not only climbers, but also tall-growing herbaceous plants, trees and shrubs and certain vegetables.

Ivies and Virginia creeper are self-clinging and will cover a wall without any help, whereas clematis, honeysuckle and climbing roses need some kind of supporting framework. Depending on how much space you wish to cover and the shape in which you want the plants to develop, you can select from various wooden, plastic or plastic-covered metal trellises in several designs. Or you could use horizontal wires attached to vine eyes to achieve the same result. Whichever you use, they must all be 5–8cm/2–3in away from the wall to allow air to circulate.

In the borders, tall-growing herbaceous perennials such as delphiniums, lupins and helianthus will need supporting. You can use canes and twine in summer, but you will obtain a more natural effect by using pea sticks in the shape of a wigwam. These must be put in position while the plants are short so that they grow through them. There are proprietary supports comprising circles of wire mesh on legs which do the same job or, if growth is more advanced, you could use L-shaped Link-Stakes which loop together around the plant.

Runner and climbing French beans need bamboo canes or bean poles to climb up; alternatively, you could use strong twine or nets. And you'll only get a good crop of garden peas if you keep them upright by growing them up nets or pea sticks. *FD*

T O O L B O X

U S E F U L   G A D G E T S   F O R   S U M M E R

THREE-PRONGED HOE

The tool I use most during the summer is a hoe with three bent, downward-facing prongs. It's ideal for keeping the weeds in check between the rows of vegetables. All I have to do every week is walk backwards, scuffling the soil with it as I go. In the flower borders the bedding plants are in irregularly shaped groups, no straight rows, and I also use it to go round these. If I happen to catch one of the plants, it's just pulled out without doing any damage and so can be replanted. *FD*

SHEEP SHEARS

The summer jobs I enjoy most are snipping and clipping, but instead of struggling with the usual blunt kitchen scissors or secateurs (which aren't much good for soft material), I use a small pair of sheep shears. A really sharp, good-quality pair is so pleasing to use that snipping is almost addictive. The garden has never looked neater. I even dead-head things that, pre-sheep shears, I'd have turned a blind eye to. *SP*

LONG-HANDLED WEED FORK

My borders are so closely planted that it is difficult to walk between the plants easily, and yet still the weeds appear. I found the perfect tool in a local ironmongers' – a stainless steel weeding fork on a very long handle, which is first-rate for lifting out young interlopers without harming surrounding specimens or running the risk of treading on something precious. I never walk round the garden without it, and it's excellent for leaning on to survey the fruits of my labours! *DL*

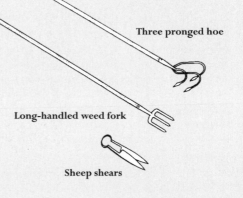

Three pronged hoe

Long-handled weed fork

Sheep shears

CONTAINER-GROWN
STRAWBERRIES

ONE OF THE highlights of summer is to go out and pick strawberries from your own garden. But what do you do if you are short of space for after all the plants take up a good deal of ground all year round and yet have a short cropping season? Granted, you can pick strawberries right through to the autumn by growing different varieties, but then you'll be using even more room. So what's the answer? Grow them in containers. There is a range of these on the market – plastic towers, terracotta pots, barrels, all with planting holes in their sides. Starting at the bottom, plant these up, using soil-based compost such as John Innes No. 3 and popping in a plant every time you reach one of the holes, finishing off with several in the top.

Or you can make your own by building a three-tier 'wedding cake' out of split logs or plastic mesh lined with polythene. Make three circles 90cm/3ft, 60cm/2ft and 30cm/1ft in diameter, all 20cm/8in deep. Build them up, one on top of the other, filling them with good compost as you go, Then plant nine, six and three plants round the edge of each one respectively, giving you a total of eighteen plants in one square metre/yard. They can also be grown in hanging baskets and window boxes, but whatever type of container you use, they must be fed with a high-potash liquid feed throughout the growing season and given plenty of water as the compost must never be allowed to dry out. *FD*

NOTES

WATERING WISDOM

Plants need water to survive, but their needs vary greatly — a species with succulent leaves capable of storing water obviously requires less than one indigenous to a moist area. To cut down on watering, it is always best to start by choosing the right plant for the situation. Under normal conditions, an established ornamental garden does not need regular watering. Mulching will help to conserve existing soil moisture even in a long period of drought, and a soil rich in organic material will remain damp longer than one lacking in humus.

Automatic drip system

As a rule, the roots of mature plants are able to search for water during a dry spell. However, young or recently transplanted ones will not have a root system able to cope for more than a short time and it is particularly important that they should not become dehydrated. Vegetable and fruit crops may also suffer if they receive insufficient water — although the plants may not die, they can become tough, woody or unpalatable, and fruit trees and bushes may abort some or all of their crops.

If you have to water, always give a good soaking — just dampening the soil can do more harm than good because it can cause roots to grow towards the surface. A thorough drenching once or twice a week is far better than a daily dribble. It is easier to judge how much water you are giving if you use a can rather than a hosepipe or sprinkler.

Always water outdoors during the evening — the soil will stay damp longer and you will avoid damaging the leaves or petals by allowing sunshine to scorch water droplets. Under glass it is wiser to water in late afternoon during summer. Cold water lying around all night can encourage diseases.

Container plants will always need more water than those growing in the open ground. Two or three times a day may be necessary in very hot weather. A more practical way of watering container plants is by an automatic drip system and timer — these are readily available at garden centres.

Try to resist watering your lawn. It may look dreadfully brown in a drought, but it will soon recover when it rains. Instead, raise the blades on your mower and leave the clippings on as a mulch. *DL*

NOTES

Hesperis matronalis
PLANT PORTRAIT

*H**esperis matronalis*, also known as damask violet, dame's violet or sweet rocket, is a hardy perennial growing 60–90cm/2–3ft tall, with spikes of single lilac, purple and white flowers which are deliciously scented during the evening – hence its name, from the Greek *hesperos*, meaning 'evening'. It has a long flowering period, and is easily raised from seed. Originally a native of southern Europe, it was introduced to Britain in the late sixteenth century and has been a popular cottage-garden flower ever since. In some areas it has even become naturalized in grass verges.

Hesperis matronalis 'Lilacina Flore Pleno' is a particularly beautiful double-flowered lilac form resembling in some respects a dainty double stock. Although perennial, like its close relatives the wallflower and stock, the plant rapidly becomes woody, and should be regularly renewed from cuttings. Unlike single forms, it does not come true from seed.

Single forms of *Hesperis matronalis* are easily grown in moist but well-drained soil, but 'Lilacina Flore Pleno' is more exacting in its requirements, and should be planted in moist, sandy loam to which some leaf mould has been added. It is an ideal companion for lillies, and a delightful subject for a scented garden. *DL*

NOTES

GARDENER'S TIP

In herb beds, over-rich soil and too much water are undesirable. But keep herb plants clean; squirt with water weekly to wash off dust and dirt (especially in hanging baskets or windowboxes near busy roads), and pick them over by hand to remove pests like greenfly and any yellow or damaged leaves.

SUMMER HERB CARE

Summer cooking needs a regular supply of home-grown herbs. So good routine care – whether your plants are in pots, hanging baskets, windowboxes, the edges of beds, or in a proper herb garden – is well worth the trouble.

Herbs need a warm, sunny, sheltered spot to develop their full flavour. Most are Mediterranean plants that thrive naturally in dryish conditions and poor soil – these conditions also help to concentrate the essential oils. When growing herbs in pots or other containers, use soil-based compost (John Innes No. 2) and avoid over-watering or heavy feeding – a weekly quarter-strength tomato feed after plants have been in the same compost more than three months is all that is needed.

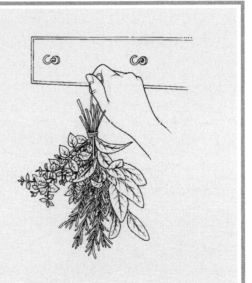

Nip out the tips of perennial herbs like bay, rosemary and sages regularly to keep the plants bushy – dry the bits if you can't use them in cooking at once. I cut my chive plants to a couple of centimetres/an inch above the ground any time during the summer when old foliage becomes too floppy or the flowers are over, to keep plants looking tidy. I also like to sow short-lived herbs like chervil and basil little and often – the leaves lose all their taste once flower buds form (which they do within a few weeks in summer). A fresh sowing every month keeps the kitchen well supplied. *SP*

NOTES

CHOICE CONTAINER

LARGE TUB FOR THE PATIO

MY FAVOURITE PATIO container is a half-barrel. These are widely available, long-lasting and comparatively inexpensive, and the timber and style blend well with just about every kind of domestic architecture, garden design and hard landscaping.

The larger the half-barrel, the greater the impression it creates. One 60cm/2ft in diameter will be quite spectacular when in full flower. For maximum impact, I like to plant closely, but try to bear in mind that although all young bedding plants start off more or less the same size, some will be considerably bigger than others by the middle of the growing season. A spacing of 5–8cm/2–3in for moderate-growing species and 10–15cm/4–6in for stronger ones works quite well.

The white walls and thatched roof of our cottage favour a good old mixture of colours, but a scheme of single or co-ordinating colours can be just as exciting.

The wooden sides of the barrel look quite attractive if left unclothed, but I still feel that some pendulous varieties cascading over the edge create a better effect. *Plectranthus* (Swedish ivy), *Glechoma hederacea* 'Variegata' (trailing nepeta), variegated ivies, *Lotus berthelotii*, trailing lobelia, *Helichrysum petiolare* and *H. microphyllum*, ivy-leaved pelargoniums and 'Surfinia' petunias are useful for this. Two other container plants which have become very popular in recent years, *Scaevola* 'Blue Fan' and *Bidens* 'Golden Goddess' also have a strong, spreading habit, and so need to be placed near the edge.

I like a good centre point, such as an upright-growing fuchsia like 'Swingtime', one large or three smaller plants, or osteospermum. The space in between is filled with bushy bedding plants like zonal pelargoniums, felicia, brachycome, *Begonia semperflorens*, annual dianthus, gazanias, dwarf zinnias and French marigolds. Of course, not all these will fit into one barrel. Try to use several of each species, so that the container doesn't look too bitty. The wide range of plants makes it easy to ring the changes from year to year. *FD*

D R A W I N G   B O A R D

A   N E W   L A W N

Levelling soil

❦ Clear the site, removing any rubble, large stones and other debris. If it's overgrown with weeds, spray with a weedkiller containing glyphosate, following the instructions on the container.

❦ Dig the ground over or even trench it, forking over the subsoil to improve drainage. If the soil is heavy, incorporate large amounts of gravel to open it up.

❦ Give the ground time to settle, but fork through it occasionally to disturb any germinating annual weeds and remove the roots of perennial ones that you missed when digging.

❦ Good drainage is important, so check the area after periods of heavy rain. If water stands for any length of time, it may be worth considering installing a drainage system.

❦ If you don't want humps and hollows, the site should be level. Use pegs, a straight edge and a spirit level to achieve this, distributing the topsoil evenly.

❦ Work out how many square metres of turf or what quantity of seed is required. Measure the whole area; don't allow for curved edges or beds, as these are best cut out later.

❦ April and September are the best months to sow, but turf can be laid at any time as long as ground conditions are favourable. Apply a base fertilizer a week before doing either of these jobs.

❦ Choose a fine day to sow a lawn. Rake the soil into a fine tilth, mark out the site into square metres or yards, sow the seed at 40–55g/ 1½–2oz per square metre/yard, then rake lightly to cover it.

❦ If you are using turf, buy the best quality you can afford. Lay a row, then work from boards laid on top of these, moving them as you go. The turves should be touching and the joints staggered, like bricks.

❦ If the weather is dry, seed will be slow to germinate and the turves will shrink and curl at the edges, so if necessary apply water using a sprinkler. *FD*

Laying turf

NOTES

CLASSIC CLIMBER

THE TROPAEOLUMS

Mention tropaeolums and most people think first of nasturtiums. *Tropaeolum majus* is certainly at home in virtually any garden. Grow it in beds and borders, marching out across gravel in the style that Monet used at Giverny, over 'problem' banks or in containers – it is perfect for the new long dangly-look hanging baskets.

What 'climbing' nasturtiums won't do naturally is climb – they are actually trailers. Plant at the top of a bank and let them grown down, or tie them to netting. Give nasturtiums a sunny spot in poor dryish soil and they flower wonderfully all summer; if it is over-nourished, all you'll have is giant leaves and no bloom.

Nowadays nasturtiums come in more colours than just the traditional orange; you can find yellow, mahogany, cream, scarlet, gold, cherry and tangerine – the compact cultivar 'Alaska' has variegated foliage, too. But my favourite is the old 'Empress of India', a non-trailer with deep velvety orange-red flowers set against purplish foliage.

Wonderful though nasturtiums are, there are other tropaeolums worthy of notice, too. Canary creeper (*T. peregrinum*) is a useful self-clinging climber for trellis or hanging baskets – stems shin up the supports creating a 3-D display of fragile foliage studded with pale yellow moth-like flowers. The hardy flame flower (*T. speciosum*) is tricky to establish – even the right climate (cool, moist summers and mild winters) and conditions don't necessarily spell success. But if you have moist, well-drained, peaty soil in a mild humid area, and plant under bushes for the stems to climb up through, have a go.

Or try *T. tuberosum*, a near-hardy kind with weird egg-like tubers at soil level, and bright orange-red tubular flowers without petals – if you are lucky. I get better results with *T. tricolorum* in the greenhouse, it's a late-winter grower with similar flowers on spindly stems in spring. It looks great growing through the staging or among other climbers. *SP*

DEAD-HEADING ROSES

THE OBJECT OF dead-heading roses is twofold – to tidy up the plants by removing faded blooms and to encourage the bushes to produce new shoots to flower later in the summer.

Many varieties of Hybrid Tea, floribunda and climbing rose produce hips, often large, after flowering. Removing the spent heads ensures that the rose concentrates on making a further flush of flowers instead of channelling its energies into seed production. However, some modern varieties do not produce hips; instead the flower head and stalk below just wither and eventually drop off down to the first leaf.

Traditional rosarians dead-head their roses in a specific way. They remove the dead flower head and its supporting stem down to the first true compound leaf – that is, one with five leaflets – or the first outward-growing true leaflet (which should produce an outward-pointing new shoot), or even to an outward-facing leaf about half-way down the current season's stem. This, it is said, is to preserve the good shape of the bush, keep the head open to reduce disease and assist with the main pruning in the winter. In fact, this method has the disadvantage that the bush takes longer to flower again, and it does little to help with either disease prevention or winter pruning. It has now been found that rose bushes which are dead-headed merely by removing the old flowered shoot down to the first leaflet, or even by just clipping off the spent heads, produce a further, often more prolific, flush much more quickly, with little or no detriment to the plant. With many modern, repeat-flowering varieties, even leaving on the spent heads does not prevent new flowering shoots being produced, although the bushes may look less neat in the meantime. DL

Above left: **dead-heading roses the conventional way**
Above right: **dead-heading roses – modern practice**

NOTES

FORCING BULBS FOR CHRISTMAS

CERTAIN THINGS remind me of Christmas – the smell of the needles on the tree, the turkey cooking, the brandy on the pudding and, as I go downstairs in the morning, the perfume from the hyacinths and the unmistakable scent of 'Paper White' narcissi in the porch.

To have hyacinths flowering for Christmas, you need to plant prepared bulbs – those that have been given a false winter to bring the flowering period forward. They should be planted in the last week of August or the beginning of September, placed somewhere dark and cold and they should never be allowed to dry out. Many people plant them straight into the bowls and more often than not they obtain a good display. I prefer to plant them in individual 9cm/3½in pots of John Innes seed compost and, after watering them, stand them outdoors in a plunge bed, covered with 10–12cm/4–5in layer of moist pulverized bark. I bring them into the warmth at the end of November after checking to make sure that the flower buds are visible among the leaves. If not, they go back outdoors and are checked again a week later. When they

are 10–12cm/4–5in high and I can tell how tall they are going to grow, they are planted in the bowls. I adjust them in the compost so that the tops are all the same height.

'Paper Whites' are very easy to grow; just plant them in bowls and put them in a cool, light place where they will flower eight to nine weeks later. *FD*

NOTES

COLLECTING SEED

MORE AND MORE people are saving seed from their own plants. And not just to cut gardening costs. Some save seed of perennials or rock plants to donate to one of the specialist plant society seed-exchange schemes; in return, donors can draw out more packets than usual. Others save seed of favourite plants to give friends, or to preserve heirloom varieties from extinction.

So which seeds are worth saving? Botanical species are good candidates – named varieties of shrubs, herbaceous flowers and rock plants don't come true from seed. Also worth saving are open-pollinated sweet peas and vegetable varieties; these are mainly older varieties, and have been selected over many generations to come true from seed. In contrast, seed taken from F_1 hybrids produces a huge mixture of inferior offspring.

Seed-saving techniques vary somewhat between species; consult a good book on plant propagation if you are a serious seed-saver. But as a general rule, collect tree and shrub seed just before it is ripe, wash well, and sow immediately. Let alpine, perennial and annual flower seed ripen and dry in the pod, then separate seed from husks and store in paper envelopes to sow in spring. (Many alpines are best sown when ripe.)

Vegetables need care to avoid cross pollination. Grow beans for seed 100 metres or yards away from others of the same species, and prevent cuckolding of cucurbits by 'pegging' female flowers shut and then hand-pollinating with a male flower of the same cultivar before re pegging. Root crops don't flower till their second year – lift roots in autumn, store well for winter, then replant next spring and let seed heads mature. Store vegetable seed in paper bags in a cool, dry place at a steady temperature – don't store peas and beans in sealed containers, or an internal fungus prevents germination. *SP*

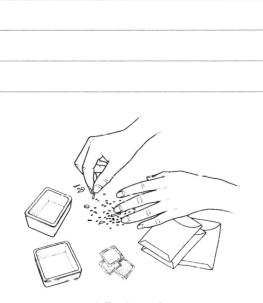

Collecting seed

GOOD COMPANIONS

ONIONS AND CHUMS

Nowadays, gardeners who know their onions are growing them in summer flower borders. Ornamental allium heads have strong globular shapes that contrast brilliantly with herbaceous spires and spikes. Grow them in groups between low spreading perennials or in front of tall earlier-flowering kinds to mask the old foliage. Any well-drained soil and sunny situation suits them.

The huge *Allium giganteum* with 10cm/4in lilac flowers on 1.2m/4ft stems is the one to go for in a big border; elsewhere choose short-stemmed *Allium christophii* with metallic 20cm/8in spheres for a similarly spectacular effect. Sophisticated *Allium siculum* has heads of nodding greenish flowers that look great with hosta foliage, while *Allium sphaerocephalum* is one most garden centres stock – plant in clumps among herbaceous flowers for masses of small mauvish 'blobs'.

And although ornamental onions set the trend, now other summer bulbs are fast joining their ranks as seasonal border highlights. Some are sensational. Try a trio of acidanthera (60cm/2ft high, with perfumed maroon-centred white flowers: grow them in groups), galtonia (summer hyacinth – tall spikes of white or greenish bell flowers) and eucomis (pineapple flower, with green and white mini-pineapples on sticks). Tigridias have flamboyant three-cornered flowers in hot fluorescent colours; they are the perfect answer for livening up a tired sunny spot.

Lilies are old favourites, now seeing a new lease of life in containers – the ideal way to grow them if your garden soil is not suitable. Simply plunge them to the rim anywhere you want to add a splash of instant colour. So make onions – and their chums – the stars of your summer border. *SP*

NOTES

S U M M E R   C H E C K L I S T

❦ Planting of summer bedding should be completed by mid-June – by now it's safe to put in even the most tender plants.

❦ It's already time to be thinking of next year's spring display. Biennials such as wallflowers, forget-me-nots and *Bellis* daisies need sowing in an outdoor seed bed if they are to make good bushy plants to go out in the autumn.

❦ Certain jobs need doing throughout the summer. Dead-head annuals, perennials and roses as soon as the flowers fade. Keep an eye open for pests and diseases and spray at the first sign. Water containers daily even if it rains, although plants in the open ground will only need some if it's very hot and dry (if so, give them a thorough soaking). All plants, especially those in containers, will benefit from a liquid high-potash feed every two or three weeks.

❦ Clip evergreen hedges before they get out of hand. Fast-growing ones such as privet will need thinning three or four times during the season to keep them looking neat and tidy.

❦ Mow lawns once or twice a week, depending on how fast they are growing. If you trim the edges every time, it will give that finished look.

❦ Propagate strawberries by pegging down the runners of healthy plants into the ground or into pots of soil-based compost.

❦ Blight can ruin a crop of potatoes, so protect them by spraying them with a copper-based fungicide in early summer.

❦ If clumps of bearded iris are becoming overcrowded and too large for their allotted space, divide them at the end of the flowering season.

❦ Use non-flowering, disease-free shoots of zonal pelargoniums (geraniums) as cutting material to increase your stock. They will root readily outdoors.

❦ Sow spring cabbage in an outdoor seed bed if you want early greens next spring.

❦ As soon as crops have been harvested, prune summer-fruiting raspberries and blackcurrants. Cut back the growths that have already carried fruit down to their base.

❦ Plant colchicums and autumn-flowering crocus as soon as they become available in the shops to ensure that they will flower later in the year. *FD*

SUMMER STRAWBERRIES

Propagate strawberries by pegging down the
runners of healthy plants into the ground or
into pots of soil-based compost

Autumn

∞

THE ABILITY TO see ahead and plan your garden accordingly is one of the most elusive of gardening's arts. In a phrase with which I am particularly pleased, I once described garden design as painting in four dimensions and it is indeed time, the fourth dimension, that renders the whole task so difficult. But every other aspect of gardening must inevitably take account of time, too, for we are dealing constantly with living things in a dynamic interrelationship with their environment. Plants do not stop growing because we choose to go on holiday and it is often very hard (or expensive) to make up later for jobs put aside or forgotten some months earlier.

Good gardens begin with good soil and I don't mind how often I say it, but the key to good soil is careful cultivation and plenty of organic matter. The oft-mentioned organic matter can take almost any form that you choose (or have available) — manure, compost or pulverized bark — but fork it into the vegetable plot or new ornamental bed as you do your rough autumn digging; the worms and the winter weather will then break it down and improve the soil's structure in the process. And I do mean rough digging — remove perennial weeds, but don't worry too much about the annuals provided they are turned under, and leave the soil in large clods. Breaking down soil to a fine tilth at this time of year is so much wasted effort, for the winter rains will pound the small particles into an impervious capping.

Many garden trees and shrubs have a rich crop of seeds that can be sown now with fair expectation that winter's chill will break their dormancy and encourage them to germinate in the spring. Layer a few centimetres of sand in the base of a shallow pan, place the ripe seeds on top and then cover them with a further layer of sand. Place a sheet of newspaper over and bury the whole in a corner of the garden until the end of winter (don't forget to mark the spot). In spring, it should be unearthed and brought into warmth. SB

A PLUG FOR PLUMS

There has been a renewed interest in growing fruit, including plums, over the last few years, and many of the varieties grown in the past are being reintroduced. They may be a little difficult to track down, but any stockists will be listed in that invaluable publication, *The Plant Finder*.

You won't have any trouble buying the variety 'Victoria', as it's still one of the most popular plums around, although it was first introduced over 150 years ago. It's self-fertile and yet will still pollinate most of the other varieties nearby. The juicy, sweet fruits, yellow flushed with red, can be cooked, but they are also delicious eaten straight from the tree.

Many varieties were introduced in the early 1800s. The dessert plum 'Kirke's' or 'Kirke's Blue' has sweet, dark purple fruits but is not self-fertile, and is not suitable for growing in the north; even in the south it prefers the warmth of a south-facing wall.

'Denniston's Superb' is very similar to a gage in looks and flavour, as the fruits are pale green with a darker streak. It's a good pollinator, but it can be grown on its own and it also crops well in the north.

A plum that used to be used a good deal for bottling because of its rich, prune-like flavour is 'Diamond', although nowadays this is used

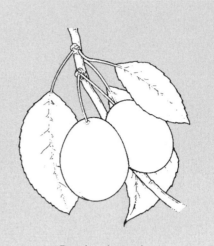

Denniston's superb

mainly as a cooker. The fruits are very dark blue, almost black, and are ready for harvesting at the end of August into September.

There are two good varieties of dessert plum that go back to the eighteenth century: 'Angelina Burdett' produces round, dark purple fruits that ripen in September. 'Coe's Golden Drop', another old favourite, has yellow fruits dotted red, which are sweet and juicy, with a slight apricot flavour.

So don't just go for new varieties, try some of the older ones as well; I'm sure you won't be disappointed. *FD*

NOTES

Autumn Gentians
PLANT PORTRAIT

There's no finer autumn-flowering alpine than the gentian. There are one or two species, including *Gentiana sino-ornata* and *G. farreri* and many hybrids worthy of planting in the garden, but if I had to choose just one, it would be *G. sino-ornata*. Its trumpet-shaped flowers are 6cm/2½in long, a rich royal blue, striped alternatively with deeper blue and with green-yellow inside and outside the tube. They are produced singly on the ends of low, spreading stems and, because they are held upright, it's very easy to see and admire their true beauty. They prefer a moist, rich organic soil which is slightly on the acid side and they resent being planted in full sun; ideally they should be in dappled shade, close to small-leaved shrubs.

Gentiana ternifolia is very similar to *G. sino-ornata* and likes the same conditions; it doesn't grow as vigorously, although if you can get it established, it will flower profusely. The flowers of this one aren't quite as deep a blue – they are paler inside the trumpet, and outside they are green-white with deep blue stripes.

If your soil is alkaline you can still grow gentians, as long as you choose *G. farreri* or any of the crosses with this as its main parent. When fully open the flowers are bright pale blue with a white throat and violet and white striped on the outside. It likes to be out in the open in well-drained soil, but it mustn't be allowed to dry out during the growing season. Yes, almost every garden would be enriched by a clump of vibrant blue gentians. *FD*

PERENNIAL PROBLEMS

Given the right situation – by which I mean a warm, sunny, sheltered spot with rich, well-drained but moisture-retentive soil – perennials virtually grow themselves. Problems usually occur when conditions are poor. In this case, choose plants that suit the conditions you have – moisture-loving plants for damp or heavy clay soils and drought-tolerant types for hot dry soil. The choice of plants with different preferences is very wide.

Some perennials have problems of their own. Peonies don't flower if planted too deeply – the crown should be only 2cm/1in below the surface. Bearded iris won't flower unless their rhizomes receive direct sun – plant them so the top half of each rhizome is above ground, and avoid growing them behind other flowers which will shade them.

But what all perennials suffer from is old age. After three years, or in the case of slow-growing kinds, five – when clumps look congested and flowering declines – they need rejuvenating. This is more easily done with plants than their minders. In early spring, dig up old clumps and divide them; use two garden forks back to back to prise them apart. Discard the centre of the clump, where growth is oldest, plus any unhealthy bits. Split the remainder into small portions. Replant after preparing the ground with organic matter and some fertilizer. *SP*

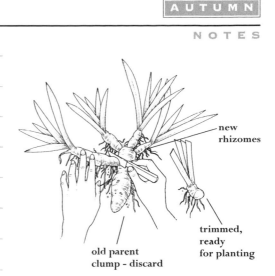

new
rhizomes

trimmed,
ready
for planting

old parent
clump - discard

GARDENER'S TIP

To improve conditions for
perennials add grit and
organic matter to heavy soil
or make raised beds; on
fast-drying sandy soil dig in
organic matter deeply
when making a new bed,
then mulch thickly in both
spring and autumn. On
windy sites, compact plants
are safest. Tall, brittle
plants like delphiniums
need staking even in
sheltered spots.

NOTES

CHOICE CONTAINER

THE STRAWBERRY POT

HIGH-RISE CONTAINERS provide the answer to making the most of a tiny space, and of the selection available, strawberry pots are by far the most elegant. Forget plastic substitutes. The classic strawberry pot is the only one to go for – a terracotta urn with scooped-out planting pockets in the sides, allowing all but the base of the container to be useful cropping space. By setting one plant per pocket plus four in the top, you can pick as many strawberries from your back doorstep as would normally need a bed 2 metres or yards square. And you can more easily protect fruit from birds, slugs and rots.

But strawberry pots are not just for growing strawberries. I like them for herbs, which do very much better in strawberry pots than in the cramped half-sized versions sometimes sold as herb pots. There is room for a complete collection of culinary herbs; I put annual kinds like parsley in the pockets and perennials like rosemary in the top.

Or why not experiment with annual flowers? A mixture of compact kinds make an interesting multi-storey display packed in pockets instead of clumped in a conventional container. The terracotta background specially suits sun-loving mesembryanthemum and portulaca.

Or plump for trendy tender perennials like gazania – the planting pockets allow you to keep named varieties separate, so it's easy to tell which is which when it's time to take cuttings in late summer. Compact rock plants make a good display in a strawberry pot, too. Evergreen kinds like saxifrages, sempervivums and *Sedum spathulifolium* make a good year-round display that takes little attention but receives plenty. Truly, strawberry pot is one of gardening's misnomers. *SP*

SOAPBOX

ARE WE ADDICTED TO POWER TOOLS?

Nowadays there is a powered gadget for every job. You can tell techno-holic gardeners instantly by their wreath of electric cables, of exhaust fumes, and rising decibels from a collection of mowers, trimmers, rakers, shredders, cutters, suckers and blowers fit to deafen you. But do we really need them?

All those gizmos are expensive. (Wouldn't you rather spend the money on plants?) They are fiddly to clean, and need storing and maintenance. You need protective clothing to use them. And they always go wrong just when you need to tidy the garden in a hurry and the shops are shut.

Quicker to use? Who are you kidding? Low-tech gardening is not only 'greener' but in most cases cheaper, faster and more convenient then a shed full of machinery.

Pocket-handkerchief-sized lawn? A hand mower does the job in less time than it takes to unroll an electric cable. Beds to edge? It's less trouble to use long-handled shears – in any case, electric gadgets demand the perfectly made lawn edges that most of use don't have. For cutting rough grass, try a scythe – it's very therapeutic. And sheep shears are fun to use for clipping, trimming, deadheading and 101 other odd jobs. If you have hedges at the back of a border, clipping by hand with shears saves wrecking your flowers when cables are dragged over them. And for preparing new ground, a spade does a better job than a rotary cultivator in almost every case – try a long-handled one, it's less tiring. Anyway, a bit of honest effort is good for you – you'd pay a fortune to exercise like that at a gym. And I bet any hand tool will outlast the equivalent power gizmo by many generations.

Sure, power tools do have their uses – if you have to manage a huge garden single-handed, or have a big workload for one particular kind. But most of us are being oversold on machinery and our gardens over-powered by technology – so let's pull the plug on it where we can. *SP*

LATE COLOUR IN THE BORDER

THE HOT DRY summers of the last few years have made mid-season flowers 'go over' sooner than usual, leaving a lot of people with prematurely empty-looking borders. My solution is simply to plant more autumn flowers to plug the gap. Chunky chrysanths contrast well with slender schizostylis (Kaffir lily), with their curvy gladiolus-like spikes in red, pink or white. Dahlias are traditionally grown in a special bed of their own, as the bigger varieties tend to swamp more delicate neighbours. But for a change, I team modern compact cultivars with penstemons, *Argyranthemum foeniculaceum* and shrubby *Salvia fulgens* and *S. grahamii* – all of which have long flowering seasons – for a slightly tropical touch.

Roses put on a good late show too, especially modern bush and cluster-flowered kinds (alias Hybrid Teas and Floribundas), though I'm not so keen on them. I prefer old-fashioned roses; 'Old Blush China' – the original 'last rose of summer' – is the best of all for late flowering.

Bedding plants can be useful; although hardy annuals are over by midsummer, most half-hardies – when well cared for – flower continuously right up to the first frost. (Tip: make a late sowing in May to have a few spares for filling gaps or replacing casualties in mid or late summer.)

I'm also beefing up borders with more late flowers like Japanese anemone, rudbeckia, diascia, red hot pokers, liriope, muscari, cimicifuga and the shrubby Russian sage (*Perovskia*). But avoid traditional Michaelmas daisies if mildew is a problem; other perennial asters such as *Aster amellus*, *A. ericoides* and *A. x frikartii* are less bothered. I reckon a good autumn display will add an extra two months of colour to the garden – as good as moving to a warmer climate, but cheaper! *SP*

PRUNING EVERGREENS AND TOPIARY

Anyone who has a hedge that they clip several times a year to keep it neat and tidy is carrying out a form of topiary. I have a privet hedge in my garden which is trimmed on average three times a year so that the sides and top are neat and square; nothing elaborate. But there's no end to the shapes you could create and if you want some ideas, several of the gardens that are open to the public have evergreen shrubs trained into forms such as animals, birds, spirals, pyramids and spheres. The most suitable shrubs for this are box, yew and bay, which are quite slow growing. If you want quick results, privet will grow much faster, but of course it will need clipping more often.

However, if you want to create any of these, you must have a good deal of patience and be willing to spend plenty of time on them. It helps if you have a good eye for straight lines and curves, but if you haven't, it's best to build a wire netting frame to the desired shape, let the shrub grow through it and just cut off the growth 5–7cm / 2–3in proud of it so that eventually the wire is hidden from view.

While plants are young, it won't just be a case of clipping; you will need to do some pruning and maybe thinning as well to achieve the desired shape. You may even have to train some of the branches to grow in the right direction by tying them together with soft twine. *FD*

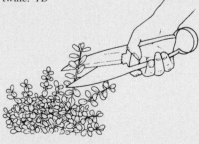

IN PRAISE OF PUMPKINS

Virtually overnight the Cinderella of the vegetable world has shot from ugly sister to star. A few years ago, all you saw of pumpkins was the occasional photo in a seed catalogue. But now, at the first hint of the panto season, greengrocers' shops are full of them, disused fireplaces are transformed into fruitful cucurbit displays, and gardeners get busy planning next year's harvest. Decoration aside, giant pumpkin contests are probably the most profitable use for pumpkins – we have never developed a taste for pumpkin pie, although pumpkin wine and soup, and roast pumpkin, are all delicious.

Home growers have a whole range of varieties to try. For cooking, smaller varieties like 'Jackpot' and 'Jack-be-Little' are most manageable. Varieties with hull-less seed like 'Triple Treat' are cultivated for 'pumpkin nuts' – eaten roasted and salted or as a health food. If you want a monster, choose 'Atlantic Giant', which can reach several hundred kilograms in weight given good cultivation. (And several hundred pounds in prize money – the world record is 1945 kg/884 lb.) Those that don't quite make the grade come in handy at Hallowe'en.

If an ornamental display is your main aim, combine true pumpkins with their close cousins, squashes, which come in all sorts of colours, sizes and shapes – from Indian clubs to pie dishes. But if you want to grow your own authentic fairy-tale coach, look out for the old French variety 'Cinderella' ('Rouge Vif d'Etampes'). Occasionally available through the heritage seed library of HDRA (the Henry Doubleday Research Association) or from sources overseas, this is the classic ribbed red fruit – straight out of a story-book. *SP*

NOTES

TREES FROM SEED

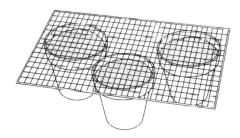

PROPAGATING TREES from seed is inexpensive and fairly easy, but it does take a little time. Some of them will germinate the year after sowing, but others need to go through two winters before they emerge. Most of the trees that are hardy in the British Isles, such as holly and maple, don't require any artificial heat, but any that originate in the warmer parts of the world will need quite high temperatures.

The seeds must be ripe and should be sown straight away, never allowing them to dry out. They can go directly into pots or trays on top of a gritty, well-drained compost. Cover them with approximately 1cm/½in of grit, water them and place them outdoors at the mercy of the weather. Or, if you want to grow several of one variety and space is limited, you can sow the seed in several layers between gritty sand in a deep container such as a 15cm/6in pot and leave them outside during the winter so that they receive a chill. (This is known as stratification.) While they are outdoors they should never be allowed to dry out; neither should they become dry or waterlogged. They are at risk from small rodents such as mice, so protect them by surrounding the container with small-mesh wire netting or, alternatively, sow them in a tin provided you make holes in the lid and the base to let in air and moisture. Then sow them in trays or a shallow drill in an outdoor seed bed in spring when the weather starts to improve.

Once germinated, the seeds should be potted up separately into 8cm/3in pots of well-drained potting compost, or, if you have room to spare in the garden, lined out in a nursery bed. Take care when handling them, holding the leaves rather than the stems or roots, as these can easily be damaged. FD

SMALL BULBS FOR ROCK GARDENS

*T*he value of small bulbs should not be forgotten for extra interest in a spring container or alpine garden.

Narcissus triandrus 'Albus', sometimes called 'Angel's Tears', reaches only 15cm/6in tall and therefore is an ideal partner for spring-flowering rock plants. The 'hoop petticoat' daffodil, *Narcissus bulbocodium conspicuus*, is ideal for a container, where the unusual and dainty flowers can be viewed closely. Botanical tulips, like the exquisite *T. biflora*, striking lilac *T. humilis pulchella*, and dainty *T. tarda*, are equally at home in an alpine garden or a trough, while those with variegated leaves, such as *Tulipa praestans* 'Unicum' and the *T. greigii* hybrids, have foliage interest as a bonus.

The flowers of the species crocuses – *C. ancyrensis* and the *C. chrysanthus* and *C. tommasinianus* hybrids – arrive in profusion early in the year. The small forms of *Allium*, the ornamental onion, such as *A. moly*, *A. murrayanum* and *A. karataviense* are so useful for taking

the spring bulb season into summer. No rock garden should be without *Anemone blanda*, available in a wide range of colours, but the lovely Glory of the Snow (*Chionodoxa luciliae*) and *Scilla campanulata* can be too invasive, for they will self-seed with wicked abandon. However, these are ideal for a windowbox, where they can be both enjoyed at close quarters and contained. *Puschkinia libanotica* will give a similar effect, only more moderately, and *Iris reticulata* has both delicate beauty and fragrance on a March day. And if you feel that *Muscari botryoides*, the grape hyacinth, is a little too run-of-the-mill, then try a more unusual species, such as the fluffy *Muscari comosum* 'Plumosum', pale blue *M. armeniacum* 'Cantab', *M. latifolium*, or the lovely *M. muscarimi*, which has everything a spring bulb should offer – delightful two-coloured flower spikes which are lilac at the top and creamy-yellow lower down, together with a sweet fragrance. *DL*

NOTES

BEDDING DOWN AND TUCKING UP BORDER PLANTS FOR WINTER

HERBACEOUS PERENNIALS are divided into three categories, the very tender ones such as argyranthemums and gazanias which have to be lifted, potted and taken under cover for the winter; *Phlox paniculata,* heleniums, hemerocallis and other very hardy subjects which can just be left to their own devices, and those in between which can be left outside as long as they are protected. Kniphofias and *Incarvillea delavayi* are two that are not totally hardy and so, more often than not, will

Perennial covered with straw held down with netting

need some protection if left outside. Of course, much depends on where in the country you live. In the warmer south you can often get away without taking any of these indoors, as long as you shelter them if temperatures drop dramatically, which doesn't happen very often. If you are in doubt as to which ones will survive outdoors in your winters, it's better to play safe.

The roots are the most important part of the plants and so a good thick mulch of garden compost, well-rotted farmyard manure or a mixture of pulverized bark and chippings will stop the frost from penetrating down to them.

The tops can be protected in several ways. The evergreen kniphofias should have their leaves pulled upright and tied together to prevent water getting into the crown and, if low temperatures are forecast, a layer of spun bonded fleece over them will ensure their safety. This is an ideal material if you are caught out, as it's easy to just drape over a plant. If you want a more permanent covering to last right through the winter, straw or dried bracken held down with netting is ideal. *FD*

NOTES

AUTUMN LEAF COLOUR

*I*t will be obvious to anyone who has ever accorded plants more than a passing glance that as they progress from seedling to senescence and ultimate death, they pass through changes that are more than simply ones of size. Leaf shape in particular often changes as plants mature and sometimes, as in species of eucalyptus, the plant is deliberately cut back annually to remove the older shoots and so encourage the formation of the more attractive juvenile foliage. The reasons for many of these differences are not known, but a very obvious one that is certainly important in gardens is the change in leaf colour that occurs in many deciduous plants as the individual leaves reach the end of their lives and senesce in autumn.

Chlorophyll production slowly ceases, so exposing other coloured pigments in the leaf, especially yellow carotenoids. Sometimes further pigments such as red anthocyanins are produced at this time, thus enhancing further the very attractive appearance of autumn foliage. At least some of these processes are temperature- as well as daylength-induced and the reason that so many North American maples and other trees fail to produce such spectacular colour in Britain can be attributed to the greater contrast between warm days and cold nights that occurs in the American Fall.

Among the very best and most celebrated plants for autumn leaf colour, of course, are the maples; and for our climate, the Japanese species and varieties are generally much better than the North American. But maples are by no means the only options and others that are perfectly suitable for relatively small gardens include the snowy mespil (*Amelanchier lamarckii*), some of the white-barked birches including *Betula jacquemontii*, the delightfully and much too infrequently planted liquidambar, some of the ornamental rowans such as *Sorbus* 'Joseph Rock', the Persian ironwood (*Parrotia persica*), hawthorns including *Crataegus prunifolia*, and ornamental apple and pear species, among which *Malus florentina* is a particular delight. *SB*

FRUIT BUSHES FOR SMALL SPACES

If you like to enjoy gooseberries or red and black currants at their dewy best, plus gourmet treats that don't travel like white currants and dessert goosegogs, the only way is by growing your own. Now space-saving shapes combined with compact varieties make it possible to fit a few fruit bushes into the tiniest garden and still get a worthwhile crop.

Even without a special fruit cage, bushes can be grown in a border (they are as pretty as flowering shrubs), in productive low hedges or large pots of John Innes No. 3 potting compost on the patio. Trained as cordons, they make great 'garden dividers'. Bush fruits are self-fertile, so you don't need to worry about partners for cross pollination. For high-yielding compact varieties, choose 'Ben Sarek' or 'Ben Connan' blackcurrants and grow them as bushes; blackcurrants are not suitable for growing as cordons or standards. No compact red or white currants exist, though 'Redstart' (red) and 'White Versailles' (white) make neat upright growth – train them as double or triple cordons flat against walls or fences.

Gooseberries are naturally sprawling and prickly bushes, but trained as cordons or standards are painless to prune and pick. If you only have room for one plant, grow a dessert variety like 'Whinham's Industry' (my favourite); thin the fruit in June and use the small green berries for cooking, then let the rest ripen to eat raw later in summer, for the best of both worlds.

And if you fancy something different, try blueberries: they make beautiful bushes for large pots of ericaceous compost if the soil is not naturally acid. Lone plants fruit well, but a pair yields more heavily due to better pollination. *SP*

PLANTING A WINTER HANGING BASKET

By now, our summer hanging baskets are looking a little sorry for themselves. Don't leave them to shrivel on the bracket over the winter, but think ahead.

Some of the perennial summer-basket plants can be carefully removed, potted up and kept in a frost-free place to re-use next summer, but as new plants can be raised or purchased so inexpensively these days, it isn't a sin to shred the contents of the old baskets and put them on the compost heap, then start afresh next spring with new materials.

Give your baskets a good scrubbing, then replant them with things to give your garden winter interest.

Solid-sided baskets are easy to plant up, but can look a little austere until the plants have grown over the edge to soften the sides. Place a thin layer of a good potting compost on the bottom, then on top of this place dwarf bulbs such as botanical tulips, crocuses and narcissi, close together but not touching. Then almost fill the basket with more compost, and plant spring bedding subjects into this. Mixing a few young evergreen shrubs in with the bedding plants will give added interest. Use trailing plants like ivy, aubrieta and arabis to disguise the sides.

Give the baskets a good watering before hanging them up again; and do remember to check that the brackets are secure. *DL*

$\mathscr{A}$ wire basket can also be planted for winter, but use a thick layer of moss or a stout liner to prevent the compost freezing rapidly during cold weather. Plant up the sides in the same way as a summer basket, but in an exposed situation, use small specimens of tough shrubs like *Aucuba japonica*, *Cotoneaster dammeri* or dwarf hebes rather than more fragile semi trailing winter pansies, aubrieta or arabis, which, being soft-leaved, can take a real battering in windy weather.

NOTES

T O O L B O X

U S E F U L   G A D G E T S   F O R   A U T U M N

BORDER FORK

Autumn is harvesting time, and this is when I wouldn't be without my well-used border fork. It has very sharp prongs and a wooden T-shaped handle which is 10cm/4 in longer than those on my other forks of this type. I use it for lifting onions, beetroot and carrots, as well as the bedding plants when they have finished. Then, before the spring-flowering biennials are planted, it's used to fork through the beds. Whenever I need a fork to use in the garden, this is the one I always reach for first. *FD*

ELECTRIC LEAF SWEEPER

For years I cleaned up fallen leaves with a brush and rake. Then I tried out a garden vacuum cleaner, which can both suck up leaves into a bag and blow them into piles, and I was converted. It is capable of sucking out debris from the most awkward corners and crevices; for the first time in my life, collecting leaves and making leaf mould is a positive delight. *DL*

PITCHFORK

If you really want some fun disguised as legitimate work, get a pitchfork. When I had a nursery years ago, we used to rot down straw bales to make compost for digging in and mulching. When it needed spreading, a pitchfork was the perfect weapon. It's best for moving fibrous material; earthy compost falls between the prongs, but if you have a compost heap made of old plant stems and similar matter it's just the job. *SP*

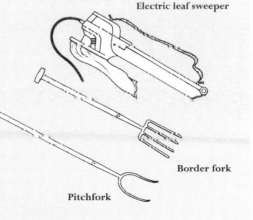

Electric leaf sweeper

Border fork

Pitchfork

CLASSIC CLIMBER

PARTHENOCISSUS SPECIES

Parthenocissus henryana is a 'must' for autumn colour, although its attractive foliage will provide interest all summer long. A member of the vine family, it is a self-clinging climber. The compound leaves comprising three to five oval leaflets are dark green or bronze with silvery-white veining, and turn a fiery red in autumn before falling. Best grown in half-shade, it will tolerate full sun, although this will make the leaves turn colour and fall much more quickly at the end of summer. In full shade, its autumn hues are far less pronounced.

The best support for *Parthenocissus henryana* is a large, blank wall, where it can be allowed to grow unchecked. Alternatively, it can be used to cover an old tree stump of adequate proportions.

The plant was originally discovered by Augustine Henry in central China around 1885, and introduced to Britain by the great plant collector Ernest Wilson. The name parthenocissus is derived from the Greek '*parthenos*', meaning virgin, and '*kissos*' – ivy – an adaption of the English name Virginia creeper. The true Virginia creeper, *Parthenocissuss quinquefolia*, originates, as its name suggests, from the eastern United States of America. But perhaps the most fiery red of all is another Chinese species, *Parthenocissus tricuspidata*.

Parthenocissus henryana requires no regular pruning, though you may eventually have to trim it around windows and doors. Young plants can be a little slow to get established; this can usually be overcome by making sure that the soil into which they are planted is rich and moist. As the area near a wall is often dry, young plants should be watered regularly if necessary – even, during dry spells, outside the growing season. There should be no difficulty in persuading it to cling, but it is best to avoid artificial means of support like trellis or wires. Instead, lay the plant down on the soil near the wall or tack it lightly to a tree stump and the new shoots should produce adhesive pads and start to climb.

Don't worry that these modified tendrils will damage the wall. There should be no problem if the brick or stonework and pointing are sound, though it may be advisable to check that the mortar is hard and the wall face in good condition, and remedy any defects before the climber becomes established. *DL*

NOTES

DRAWING BOARD

NEXT YEAR'S HERB BORDER

❦ Choose a site that gets at least six hours' sun and, if the herbs are to be used for cooking, choose a convenient position that is easily accessible from the kitchen. The soil should be well drained, yet hold sufficient moisture during the summer. Add coarse grit to heavy ground, and garden compost or well-rotted farmyard manure to soil that's light and sandy.

❦ Dig the area deeply, break up the subsoil to improve drainage and remove the roots of perennial weeds as you go; if you leave any in, they will cause problems later.

❦ The bed can be planted formally, in a shape such as a wagon wheel with each section divided by a low hedge of box or santolina, or you can design your own layout.

❦ If you prefer an informal border, remember that you will have to reach the plants for weeding and gathering, so don't make it too wide unless you place flags to use as stepping stones.

❦ Make a plan of the herbs you are going to grow and where they are to be planted, bearing in mind height, spread and whether they are annual or perennial.

❦ Mint and other invasive herbs can be restricted by planting them in functional containers which can be plunged beneath the surface of the bed, or use decorative pots and make a feature of them.

❦ Annual herbs can be started off under glass. To avoid root disturbance, sow two or three seeds to each 9cm / 3½in pot in March, harden them off and plant them out, still in their clumps. It's also possible to sow annual herbs directly outdoors *in situ* when the soil warms up in spring. Mark out each block with silver sand or a pointed stick and sow sparingly in shallow drills.

❦ Raise perennial herbs from seed, or propagate them by taking tip cuttings or by division, making sure that the parent plants are healthy. *FD*

Herb bed in the shape of a wagon wheel

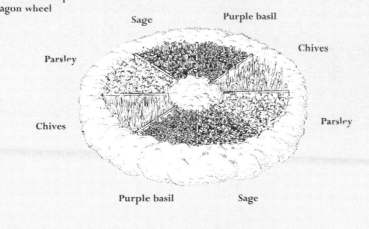

Sage

Purple basil

Parsley

Chives

Chives

Parsley

Purple basil

Sage

GOOD COMPANIONS

GLORIOUS GROUND COVER

Planting large numbers of a single species so close together that, once established, they efficiently suppress weeds is an excellent way of dealing with large areas where time for maintenance is limited. The result can be dull, however, and one may be unimpressed by the mass plantings of bomb-proof shrubs so beloved of modern developers and planners.

Ground cover does not, however, have to appear mundane to be functional. For instance, massed hostas both look spectacular and make superb weed suppressors. So do the splendid hardy geraniums, and a fantastic effect can be had from a block of, say, the green-edged, yellow *Hosta* 'Gold Standard' or blue-leaved *Hosta sieboldiana* against a drift of the deep magenta *Geranium procurrens*.

Evergreen ground cover tends to be favoured, and yet there is a great advantage in being able to clean the planted area thoroughly once a year, as is possible with these herbaceous species. Once they are under complete control, few weeds will grow during the winter period. In fact, many more or less evergreen herbaceous ground-cover subjects, like lamium (the ornamental forms of dead nettle), brunnera (perennial forget-me-not), epimedium and pulmonaria (lungwort) – all admirable for the job, either as single species or in blocks of several types – benefit from a good short-back-and-sides in early spring to remove old leaves and the debris which has collected among them during the year.

Many grasses are first-rate for smothering weeds, especially the low-growing, wiry festucas, which, if planted closely enough, will eventually produce the effect of an ornamental lawn when clipped over periodically to promote new growth. There is also a fine range of modern roses especially bred for ground-cover purposes, including the 'County' series – 'Kent', 'Essex', 'Northamptonshire' and the like – in a wide colour range and flower habit. Unlike some roses originally suggested for the purpose, which were often rampant, difficult to control, and only had one flowering period, these newcomers have all the advantages of good, repeat-flowering floribundas on a low, spreading bush, and are to be highly recommended. *DL*

Cleaning the greenhouse

Take up capillary matting

Wipe down glazing
bars with disinfectant

Remove shading from glass

A U T U M N C H E C K L I S T

❧ Tidy borders ready for winter, but don't overdo it. Leave seedheads for birds, and a strip of wildflowers round the edge of the garden in which spiders and beneficial insects will overwinter.

❧ Rake moss and 'thatch' out of lawns, then spike, top-dress with sifted topsoil (or gritty sand on clay soil) if needed, and feed with an autumn lawn fertilizer. Repair broken lawn edges.

❧ Pull out summer annuals and replace with spring bedding such as wallflowers, polyanthus and forget-me-nots. Plant biennials – Canterbury bells, foxgloves and Iceland poppy.

❧ For winter containers, plant primroses and Universal pansies with ivies, or use ericaceous compost and plant *Gaultheria procumbens*, a low creeping evergreen with large red berries.

❧ Clean out the greenhouse. Remove shading from glass, take up capillary matting (wash, dry and store for next year), wipe down staging and glazing bars with garden disinfectant.

❧ Sow a few hardy annuals such as calendula, candytuft, clarkia, larkspur, godetia and sweet peas in a cold greenhouse for planting out in a mild spell in March for early flowers.

❧ For winter and early spring colour in a cold greenhouse, grow pots of early-flowering alpines (such as saxifrages), dwarf bulbs (especially narcissus species) and violets, and bring a potted camellia indoors.

❧ Plant spring bulbs. Put a handful of grit under tulips and crown imperials when planting for improved drainage; and lay crown imperial bulbs on their sides to avoid the hollow centre filling with water.

❧ Move frost-tender plants such as pelargoniums, fuchsias and 'Surfinia' petunias into a frost-free greenhouse or conservatory for the winter unless you have rooted cuttings.

❧ Prune repeat-flowered climbing or rambler roses when the last flowers are over. Prune blackberries when they have finished cropping, by cutting the fruited stems to the ground; tie in new canes. *SP*

Winter

∞

DEPENDING ON the type of gardener that you feel you are, winter offers a range of options. It can be simply a period of rest and indulgence, of escape from the cold, of armchair gardening and listening to Classic Gardening Forum. Sometimes it provides an opportunity for working in the tingling clear winter air, there always being some worthy task that can exercise both your attention and your muscles. Above all, it offers a pause in the frenetic activity necessary when plants are in the flush of growth that enables you to view your garden in the sharper contrast that bare leaflessness allows.

A winter garden can have a special beauty of its own. I have even heard it suggested that gardens should be designed solely with winter in mind, since summer will take care of itself. There is more than a little merit in this, for if you plan a garden the other way around, for the summer, there's certainly no guarantee that there will be anything worth admiring in the cold months of the year. And the key to success in the winter depends on appreciating that the plant kingdom is divided into annuals, biennials and perennials.

Annuals have brief, if often glorious, existences but because the cold days of winter don't afford them good growing conditions, it is as seeds that they invisibly pass the winter months. Biennials are fairly thin on the ground at the best of times and though they are certainly evident in the winter garden as masses of foliage waiting to burst into bloom, they too often find winter a hardship as their exposed leaves are battered by wind and cold. So the full burden of winter appeal in the garden falls upon the perennials. What makes winter gardening so fascinating is capitalizing on the limited range of plants that *do* remain visible. Yes, summer spoils you with its multiplicity of form, shape and colour. Winter is the selective time, when only the hardiest can survive. The winter garden challenges gardener and plant to give of their best and be at their most ingenious. *SB*

MAKING AND
USING LEAF MOULD

WELL-MADE LEAF mould is very valuable for the garden. It can be dug in to improve the texture of the soil and used as a mulch to suppress weeds and conserve moisture, or you can add it to seed or potting compost instead of using peat. Best of all, it's free. However, it does take a little effort and a bit of patience. The leaves have to be collected and stacked and it can take up to two years for some of them to rot down. Ideally, beech and oak are the best to use. Larger leaves such as sycamore take longer to break down, and the veins and stalks can be a nuisance. You can also use conifer needles, but they are slow to decompose and the end product will be acidic.

All you need is a cage 1m/3ft square by 1.2m/4ft high, made by surrounding four posts with wire netting or plastic mesh. Collect the leaves and stack them in the cage, compacting each layer by trampling it down. Dry leaves don't break readily, so keep them damp; add water when you stack them and again if the weather is very dry. You will know the result is ready to use when after a year or so it turns almost black and crumbles like peat. If you are adding it to composts, it will need sieving to remove any stalks and so on, which can then be used on the open garden. Leaf mould is very low in nutrients and so is not really a substitute for farmyard manure or garden compost, and you will need to add a fertilizer to it when using it outdoors. *FD*

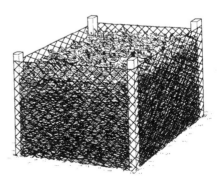

CHOICE CONTAINER

WINTER WINDOWBOX

M Y WINTER WINDOWBOXES are very important as they provide a different type of colour and style from the rest of the garden. The larger and deeper the baskets the better, but I am very successful with ones as small as 23cm/9in wide by 20cm/8in deep and 84cm/33in long. As soon as the summer bedding starts to fade, I empty my boxes and give them a good clean out, before covering the bottom with a layer of new, good-quality compost. Spring bulbs are as important as other plants – dwarf narcissi, short-stemmed hybrid and botanical tulips, garden hyacinths and species and Dutch crocus, to give a continuity of colour from mid-February until May. I am not too concerned about varieties, as long as they are suitable for container growing and have a short, stocky habit. More unusual species can be used, but they are generally more expensive and it is the overall effect that counts, not the individual. I plant bulbs close together but not touching, in layers, the largest bulbs lowest, with compost in between each layer, until the box is about two-thirds full. Then I top it off with more compost, into which I plant the rest of the display, and then wait for the succession of colour.

I keep a close watch on the watering of my boxes; being under the eaves they get little natural rainfall, and can dry out quite quickly during fine spells, even in the middle of winter. Come the spring, when the weather is warmer and they are in full bearing, they need watering more or less every day. *DL*

*I*t is essential not to choose species which grow too tall, or they can obscure much light in the house. Tall blooms are also more vulnerable to winds. Dwarf wallflowers, primroses and polyanthus, forget-me-nots and winter-flowering pansies are ideal for windowboxes – the tallest towards the back of the box, with some trailing plants like ivy and variegated periwinkle (*Vinca minor*) near the front and sides to trail over the edge. Colour can be provided throughout the season with a few ornamental kale and winter-flowering heather plants, and extra foliage effect with small plants of a bergenia that turns red or purple in winter, like 'Sunningdale', which also gives red or pink flowers in the spring.

NOTES

WINDBREAKS AND SHELTERS

Even really exposed gardens can be made to accommodate a wide range of less robust plants by first creating shelter. Where space allows, a natural windbreak of tough, fast-growing trees and shrubs can make an astonishing difference to the climate in its lee, especially if more than a few metres deep. Mountain ash, white poplar, alder, various willows, hawthorn, Swedish whitebeam, field maple, *Cornus sanguinea*, blackthorn (sloe) and hazel are among the most successful screening subjects for this purpose. Spaced close together, it should be possible to plant more delicate species in their shelter within a couple of years or so, but the windbreak should be regularly managed, coppicing some of the plants early on to create lower, bushy cover, while allowing others to grow up to form standard trees to break the wind a further distance and so protect a greater area.

This kind of shelter belt does, however, require a lot of space. In most modern gardens, there will probably only be room for a hedge. It is tempting to use a fast-growing evergreen for this purpose, such as the ubiquitous x *Cupressocyparis leylandii*, but, in fact, deciduous hedges, which filter wind rather than block it entirely, are more successful.

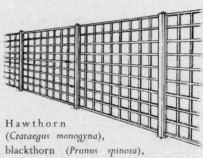

Hawthorn (*Crataegus monogyna*), blackthorn (*Prunus spinosa*), 'Myrobalan' plum and field maple (*Acer campestre*) are quick growing, but where time is not of the essence, beech and hornbeam make excellent screens.

If space (or time) won't allow for a living windbreak, it may be necessary to erect a fence or wall. Again, an open screen works better than a solid one which can create undesirable down-draughts, so use trellis fencing rather than the close-boarded kind, or pierced screen or honeycomb walling instead of a solid one. These will filter the wind rather than block it altogether, even if they are used to support climbers. If you are in a desperate hurry to plant something tender, create temporary shelter with posts and plastic windbreak netting while a more permanent and attractive living screen is maturing. *DL*

GARDENER'S TIP

Plants with berries and fruit which last well into winter are invaluable. Pyracantha, cotoneaster, holly, crab apple, mountain ash and guelder rose (*Viburnum opulus*) don't just have red-berried forms, but many good yellow-fruited varieties as well and, in the case of mountain ash, pink and white, too, which are somewhat less desirable to birds as food.

A nucleus of good, variegated evergreens will also help to dispel winter's gloom. There are excellent variegated forms of elaeagnus, laurustinus and Portugal laurel, and even the simple golden and silver privets can light up a December shrubbery.

A FRAMEWORK OF COLOUR

There is no reason why a winter garden should not be as interesting as a summer one, albeit in a different way. Although the tracery of bare branches and the delicate structure of winter flowers have their own particular charms, the finishing touches can be given through attractive evergreen foliage, stunning coloured bark or bright berries.

So many trees and shrubs have lovely bark, from the snakebark and paperbark maples, the silver birches and mahogany-coloured trunks of *Prunus serrula*, to the glowing purple, red and yellow stems of *Cornus sanguinea*, *Cornus alba* and *Cornus stolonifera* 'Flaviramea', the violet, whitewashed twigs of *Salix daphnoides*, yellow shoots of *Salix alba* 'Vitellina' and orange young wood of *Salix alba* 'Chermesina'. To see any of these through a carpet of snow can be breathtaking, and another wonderful effect is achieved with the waxy white arching stems of *Rubus cockburnianus* against bare, dark earth. If you want to plant a lime tree, choose *Tilia platyphyllos* 'Rubra', the red-twigged lime, for its bright red young shoots which stand out so well against a clear, cold winter sky.

The best berry effect in my own garden has to be the morning sun shining through the berries of *Solanum dulcamara* 'Variegata' – a versatile variegated form of woody nightshade – after rain, creating an image of diamonds topped with rubies.

The ultimate in winter interest is perhaps *Ilex aquifolium* 'Madame Briot'. With purple young shoots, leaves edged and speckled with deep gold, and a profusion of red berries in a good year, it seems to have the lot! *DL*

T O O L B O X

USEFUL GADGETS FOR WINTER

LONG-HANDLED SPADE

If I was limited to just one tool, it would have to be my long-handled spade. The original shaft broke, leaving me with a razor-sharp, forged steel blade which has been fitted on to a 1.2m/4ft length of an ash handle intended for a pitchfork. I use it for all the winter digging, for planting trees, shrubs and potatoes, for digging out 20cm/8in wide trenches for peas and broad beans, and it's also ideal for skimming the weeds off soil paths. *FD*

Long-handled spade

Chillington hoe

Folding pruning saw

FOLDING PRUNING SAW

I have two folding pruning saws, a small one, ideal for removing thin branches and rose prunings, and a larger one, with a blade able to cut quite thick material. The blades fold back into the handles when not in use, an important safety feature as both are extremely sharp. This also enables me to carry them around in my pockets so that they are always to hand when needed – which is often on my trips around the garden during the winter months. *DL*

CHILLINGTON HOE

Digging is okay, but since I discovered the Chillington hoe – a thing like a junior mattock – I hoe instead. It's a sort of big, heavy, third-world draw hoe, used with a swinging pickaxe action. The weight of the tool does all the work, so it's amazingly effortless to use. I never thought the day would come when I looked forward to heavy jobs like winter digging, clearing rough ground, smashing up clods and uprooting overgrown beds, but I do now. *SP*

NOTES

SCENT IN WINTER

IT IS SURPRISING just how may plants are blessed with superb winter fragrance, as if Nature were making up for the colder days and longer nights.

In my own garden, the first scent of winter arrives unseen, from the almost imperceptible flowers of *Elaeagnus* x *ebbingei*, whose dark green, silver-backed leaves hide an unsightly tank. This is closely followed by the lily-of-the-valley perfume from the yellow bells of *Mahonia* 'Charity' and the sweet, almost edible scent of the profusion of tufts of blush-pink flowers on a group of *Viburnum* x *bodnantense* by the fence.

These are followed after Christmas by the delicate fragrance of a witch hazel, *Hamamelis mollis* 'Jelena', with its curious 'robin's pincushions' of orange flowers on bare twigs. *Lonicera fragrantissima*, the shrubby honeysuckle, produces its perfumed waxy flowers through to early spring near the west-facing wall of the garden shed.

It would be unthinkable not to have the delicious ivory flowers of *Chimonanthus praecox*, the winter sweet, somewhere in the garden. Near by, in a sheltered corner by the garage, *Corylopsis pauciflora*, a relative of the witch hazel, takes over as the perfume from the winter sweet diminishes.

Even an awkward spot is not without scent, with a ground-cover planting of *Sarcococca humilis*. And I must not forget my namesakes the daphnes, particularly *Daphne mezereum*, and my special favourite, *Daphne odora* 'Aureo marginata'; this I keep away from winter harm in my cool greenhouse, and it amply rewards me with its fragrance while I am making my early sowings.

Early spring bulbs also give us so much in the way of scent, long before the heady perfume of the Dutch hyacinths and English bluebells. The perfume of snowdrops may not be as strong as that of *Iris danfordiae*, *I. reticulata* and *I. histrioides*, but it is nevertheless delightful. We may have to wait until spring is on its way to sample the scented delights of the many hardy varieties of narcissi that are growing in the garden, but I always make sure I have a few planted bowls of scented tazetta narcissi, such as 'Cheerfulness' and 'Hawera', so even in winter, there is spring on our cottage windowsills. *DL*

Viburnum x bodnantense

FRESH HERBS IN WINTER

FED UP WITH dried herbs that leave your dinner full of twigs? Or are you eternally buying pots or packages of fresh herbs from supermarkets? Then strike a blow for culinary independence, and grow your own. You don't even need a garden. All it takes to be self-sufficient in herbs through the winter is a warm bright windowsill indoors. Take half a dozen 9cm / 3½ in pots or old supermarket fruit punnets with drainage holes, and fill them to the rim with seed compost. Tap down gently to firm the compost, then scatter a different kind of herb seed over the surface of each container.

All the popular culinary herbs including mint, chives, basil, chervil and parsley are available as seed (through seed catalogues if not in your local garden centre) and are ideal for growing this way.

After sowing on the surface of the compost, water by standing the pots in a dish of tepid water. Then put in a large, loose plastic bag somewhere warm. When the first seedlings come through, move to the windowsill, and start cutting the seedlings as soon as they are a couple of centimetres or about an inch high. Start off a second batch in fresh pots when the 'cooking' batch is half used, to be sure of a regular supply. *SP*

*T*ry slightly unusual
kinds too, especially if
you go in for exotic
cookery – red basil,
lemon basil and
lettuce-leaf basil, leaf
versions of coriander
and dill (which are
normally grown for
their seed), and curly
mint all look extremely
pretty in pots.

S O A P B O X

FOR AND AGAINST
WINTER HEATHER GARDENS

There is just one moment in the year when I can tolerate winter-flowering heathers – when they are out in flower during the cold days of winter, especially if I can see them through the window from the warmth indoors. But every year the bed is the same – white and shades of pink and purple, sometimes just white hummocks after we have had a fall of snow. And when they have been in for a few years, they start to deteriorate and look really ragged. Once the middle of the clump has gone brown, you have to renew the plants. Whether you take cuttings or layer them, it's a case of starting again with small plants with bare earth in between until they have grown to meet one another. Granted, once established they do a very good job of covering the ground. They even help to smother some of the annual weeds, but if there are any perennial ones in there, you're in trouble and it's almost impossible to get rid of them.

I admit, heathers are easy to look after; a quick clip-over with the shears to remove the fading spikes is all that is necessary. A dressing of blood, fish and bone and a thick mulch of pulverized bark in spring and you can forget about them for the rest of the year.

But who wants a patch of green-brown porcupines all summer? *FD*

NOTES

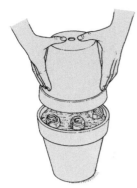

Forced chicons in a pot

FORCED FAVOURITES

WE CAN ENJOY chicory, seakale, rhubarb and certain other vegetables out of season by forcing them. The trick is to exclude light to make the shoots grow prematurely.

Lift the parsnip-like roots of chicory in November, cut back the leaves to approximately 2cm/1in from the crown, cut off the end of the root, leaving about 15cm/6in and lay them on their sides in a box of sand in a cool place. Force a few at a time by planting four or five in a 20–23cm/8–9in pot in moist compost, just leaving the crown exposed. Then place a pot the same size upside down on top of them, blocking any drainage holes to keep out the light. Place in a temperature of about 15°C/60°F until the chicons have formed, which will take three to four weeks.

We force seakale while it is still in the ground by covering each individual plant with an upturned bucket or tub. Then surround it with a thick layer of manure or compost to keep out all light and raise the temperature slightly. It will be ready to use in spring, when the blanched shoots are 20cm/8in tall. Once they have been harvested, feed and mulch the roots to build up energy for the following autumn, then you can start all over again.

You can also force rhubarb this way, but don't use the same crown every year, as it must have a rest. *FD*

THE POND IN WINTER

Because most of the garden pond is in a dormant state during winter, it can easily be overlooked, but a regular check may make all the difference between success and disaster.

Even though you may have carefully removed all the fallen leaves from the surface in autumn, it is surprising how many can blow in from other parts of the garden. January can be a month of gales, so inspect the water during windy spells, and remember that old leaves can sink quickly, so just because you cannot see any on the surface it does not mean that there are none near the bottom. Rotting leaves will quickly pollute the water – even if there are no fish in the pool, dirty water looks unsightly and unhealthy.

Aquatic and marginal plants show little signs of life at this time of year. Resist the temptation to lift, split or plant them now, as many will rot, but do examine them and remove any dead foliage, as this can also pollute the water.

If the pond freezes over completely for more than a short time, fish may die through lack of oxygen, so it is important to keep an area free from ice. A small pond heater will use very little electricity, but ensure that the water temperature is maintained slightly above freezing. Keeping the water moving will also slow down ice formation. Some people float a child's ball on the surface for this reason. Except in really low temperatures, leaving the pond pump running will also help.

Birds and other wildlife find a winter pond a useful water source, so check to see that they can have easy access – sides which slope too deeply can be fatal. Resolve to make alterations during the warmer months of the year if you feel there may be a problem here.

The metabolism of fish slows down considerably in very cold water, and so they require little to eat. However, in mild spells, if they seem to be swimming actively, they may need food, as there will be little around in the way of a natural meal. Give food a small pinch at a time, and make sure they clear it up quickly, otherwise it will decay.

If your pond looks somewhat uninteresting in winter, consider planting water hawthorn (*Aponogeton distachyos*) next summer for the following winter. Its pretty, white, fragrant flowers appear virtually year-round, but it is a strong grower, so give it space. *DL*

NOTES

D R A W I N G   B O A R D

P L A N N I N G   A   P O T A G E R

❦ Use a simple design such as those used for formal herb gardens; divide the space into segments or squares separated by paths or stepping stones for access, outlined with a formal edging.

❦ Put crops with contrasting colours, shapes or textures such as leeks and cabbages next to each other for impact.

❦ Edge paths or sunny outer boundaries with lettuce such as frilly 'Salad Bowl' and 'Lollo Rosso' or herbs like chives and parsley, where you can get at them easily.

❦ Keep taller crops like sweetcorn to the north end of the potager, not the middle, as few edible plants thrive in shade. (Remember to plant sweetcorn in a block rather than a row to ensure pollination.)

❦ Use the deep bed system for a potager – this way, plants can be positioned at close spacings so they quickly cover the ground and fill out the pattern.

❦ Choose coloured versions of everyday crops – red cabbage, purple-podded beans, golden courgettes, bull's blood beetroot (which has red leaves), and ruby chard.

❦ Scatter dill and/or nasturtium seed randomly but thinly through the potager for an informal (and edible) floral contrast with foliage crops.

❦ Grow runner beans or outdoor cucumbers on tripods of canes for maximum crops from minimum space, and to contribute vertical accents to the design. *SP*

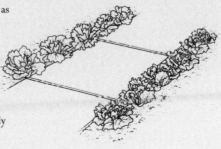

NOTES

TREES AND SHRUBS
FOR WILDLIFE INTEREST

*G*reat emphasis is placed today on planting indigenous trees and shrubs in order to encourage wildlife. Many gardens are too small to accommodate native trees like the wild cherry, so popular with birds, or the sycamore, chestnut, alder, ash, beech, birch and lime, all excellent providers of fruit, seeds or nuts as well as pollen or nectar for bees and other beneficial insects. But don't let the size of your garden worry you. Hungry birds, insects and small animals do not enquire too deeply into the origins of plants if they find something they produce is palatable, and there is no plot too small to give at least some support to wildlife.

From my kitchen window, I can watch birds devouring the berries of pyracantha, *Cotoneaster horizontalis* and a most delightful ornamental form of hawthorn, *Crataegus prunifolia*, none of which is a British native species, but all highly acceptable to wildlife. They all become alive with bees in spring when covered in their white foam of flowers. And there are few berrying trees and shrubs which birds will not touch, although some are preferred to others.

Even if a garden does not lend itself to the planting of host plants for the larvae of beneficial insects, providing them with food can help enormously. Privet flowers, lilac, lavender, berberis, ceanothus, hypericum, skimmia, senecio, spiraea, caryopteris, late-flowering hebes, gorse, ivy and, of course, buddleja are all admirable garden shrubs, and will attract bees and butterflies as a bonus.

Particularly important in the wildlife garden are shrubs which will provide pollen and nectar early in the year, when it can be scarce. On warm days in late winter, many bumble bees appear grateful for my bed of winter-flowering heathers. Around my vegetable garden is a thick screen of cheap-and-cheerful *Ribes sanguineum*, the flowering currant – not everybody's taste, and yet the noise of visiting honey bees is almost deafening.

And it should not be forgotten that, even if the bush or tree appears to have no useful purpose, it is quite likely to make a congenial habitat or shelter for some kind of wildlife – a very important consideration. Crevices in the bark will usually provide homes for a variety of insects and their larvae, which in turn could be valuable food for birds and small mammals. *DL*

Alnus glutinosa (**common alder**)

**Place seeds on top of damp tissue
in a sealed plastic container**

SEED ORDERING

To avoid being disappointed, it's essential to order your seeds early, as soon as the catalogues arrive, otherwise the most popular varieties will be sold out. But what if you have a lot of half-empty packets left over from the previous season? Gardeners are, by nature, a fairly thrifty bunch, and there is always a temptation to hang on to things. So, should these seeds be thrown away, or can they be used again the following year? Much depends on where they have been kept all winter. They are not likely to be any good if they have been left lying about on the greenhouse bench or in the garden shed or the garage, where they could get damp. The best place for them is in a screw-top jar in the salad drawer of the refrigerator.

Most flower varieties can be used a second or even a third year, and so can tomatoes and carrots. But certain types do lose their viability very quickly. Onions and lettuce, for example, are not worth saving from one year to the next. Unopened packets, particularly if they are in foil, will keep for quite a number of years, but it's always best to carry out a check with any stored seeds. Sow just a few of them in the usual way or place them on top of damp tissue in a sealed plastic container and pop them somewhere warm, such as a heated propagator or an airing cupboard. If more than 50 per cent germinate, they are worth using. If only 25 per cent come through and you've got enough seeds left, you could sow twice as many as you need; however, if it's a mixed variety you may not get the full range of colours, as the weaker ones will not have survived. If only a few sprout, it is best to order again. It's not worth sowing old seed without checking it, as you could be using valuable time, effort, compost and heat without getting any results. *FD*

NOTES

CLASSIC CLIMBER

JASMINUM NUDIFLORUM

*P*lants which flower in winter can take away much of the gloom of that time of year. There cannot be many gardens unable to accommodate the lovely winter jasmine. Seldom out of flower from late autumn to early spring in a sunny, sheltered position, its cheerful yellow flowers are as useful indoors as out. sprays brought into the house in bud will open in water and last for weeks in a cool place.

It is hard to believe that such a popular and well-loved garden plant was introduced by Robert Fortune from western China as late as 1844. *Jasminum nudiflorum* is now readily available from nurseries and garden centres, and is generally listed in plant catalogues as a climber, though it is really a shrubby species with no method of clinging by itself to a support. However, its strong, lax, spreading growth makes it ideal for training around hoops and arches, on walls and fences, or over a bank.

Regular pruning is not necessary, but plants trained on walls and other supports may have long growths shortened back each year immediately after flowering, leaving a framework of mature wood to produce the new season's shoots. It is not fussy as to position, but is unsuitable for really dense shade, where flowering will be poor. Whether or not it sheds its leaves in winter depends largely upon the weather and the position in which it is growing. In a cold spot or during a hard winter, it is largely deciduous, although its bright green stems are attractive even when the plant is not flowering.

On a warm wall or during a mild winter, however, it has the additional advantage of being more or less evergreen, and shoots pegged down into the soil in spring root readily in a matter of months to make new plants — truly an ideal winter climber. *DL*

_____

_____

_____

_____

_____

_____

_____

_____

_____

_____

THE DORMANT SEASON

THE BEST TIME to plant deciduous trees and shrubs is when they are dormant, from the end of October until the beginning of March, as long as the ground is in a suitable condition – not too wet, frozen or covered with snow. Evergreens should go in a month either side of this, while there is some warmth in the soil, as they never stop growing.

Dig the soil deeply, breaking up the subsoil to improve drainage. Add well-rotted organic matter such as farmyard manure or garden compost and a handful of bonemeal per square metre or yard. If it's very heavy, add grit. In very wet areas it may be necessary to build raised beds.

When plants arrive, get them in as soon as possible; on no account must the roots be allowed to dry out, so cover them while you are preparing the planting holes, which should be large enough to hold the roots comfortably. Before you put them in, cut off any broken branches and roots. Don't bury plants deeper than the soil mark on the stem and replace the soil, firming it down as you go. if you are moving plants, lift them with as large a root ball as possible; the best way of transporting these is on a piece of sacking or tarpaulin. The soil around the root area of a newly planted specimen must not be allowed to dry out, especially in the first summer, and remember that tall specimens need staking. *FD*

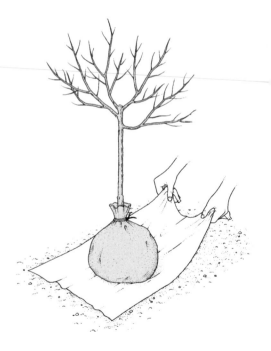

**Transporting a shrub
on a sack or tarpaulin
having wrapped the root ball
to avoid drying out**

NOTES

WEATHERPROOF CONTAINERS

Growing plants in containers is an ideal way of brightening up any dull corner. Even if you haven't got a garden, there's always room for a pot, tub or windowbox. But which of so many on the market are the best? To look right, they have to fit in with their surroundings in both style and materials. Plastic and other synthetics are fine if you have a modern house, but they don't look right alongside natural stone, where you would be better with troughs made of the local stone. Reconstituted stone is worth considering: it is versatile, comes in many attractive designs and can be a great deal less expensive than the real thing. If you have artificial paving, you can nearly always find a container to match. I don't think terracotta pots look out of place in any garden, but you must make sure that they are guaranteed frostproof if you want to leave them out all winter. Wood can be left its natural colour and varnished or treated with a wood preservative or you can change its appearance and match nearby woodwork by painting it. And try to line wooden containers with plastic sheet.

Weight is another factor to consider, especially if you want to move containers around or if you are planning a display for a roof or balcony. Plastic ones are the lightest, though are not very stable with tall plants in them, especially in windy positions. If you are using a heavy material, make sure that you put the container exactly where you want it *before* filling and planting it. But really there's no end to what you can use. You only need to look around and you'll find chimney pots, sinks, wheelbarrows – in fact anything that will hold

PLANT LABELS

OUT IN THE garden I regard plant labels as a necessary evil. I can tolerate them in the vegetable patch at the end of all the straight rows, but there's nothing attractive about them in the flower border. However, if you have hundreds of plants in a bed or are an inveterate plant collector, labels are the only sure way of knowing exactly what the varieties are. You could draw up a plan, which is fine for the larger trees and shrubs but isn't very accurate for a mass of plants in a small area, such as alpines in a rockery.

When it comes to labels, there are plenty to choose from, one factor is how long you want them to last. Wooden labels have a limited life, even if you paint them white and write on them with soft, black-leaded pencil. Those made from plastic will last a few years, but you must use a marker pen to write on them and in time they will go brittle and break, and the writing will eventually fade. One advantage of plastic is the wealth of shapes and sizes, so that you can make your choice according to how much information you want them to hold. I use a labelling machine which takes various

widths of tape. It prints different sizes of letters and if you want to colour-code your plants, you can use different coloured tapes. I just peel off the backing and stick the tape on the label. Whenever I want to change it, I just take if off and put a new one on. This is ideal from one year to the next for vegetables and annuals which are always changing. If you want something more permanent, you can use metal labels, which last for years.

Finally, if you really don't like the look of your labels, you can always push them into the soil so that they are hardly visible. *FD*

Algerian iris and winter aconite
PLANT PORTRAIT

*T*he lovely, fragrant Algerian iris (*Iris unguicularis*) is a gem for the winter garden. Formerly known as *Iris stylosa*, its flowers, about 8cm/3in across, are produced from November to March on short stalks through narrow, grass-like leaves from a rhizome-like rootstock. The flowers of the species are lavender-blue, but there are variations in colour, including a white form. It succeeds in poor, well-drained soil in a sunny position and is an ideal subject for the base of a south wall where you can allow it to grow undisturbed for many years.

The winter aconite (*Eranthis hyemalis*) is a wonderful harbinger of spring. Its buttercup-like bright yellow flowers, which grow larger in moist soil than in dry conditions, appear on short stems with the snowdrops in February and March, and it is an excellent subject for naturalizing in semi-wild, woodland areas or in shrubberies where it can grow without disturbance. In leaf-mould-rich soil, *Eranthis hyemalis* will spread both by tubers and through seed, but new colonies can be tricky to establish, and it is better to move plants 'in the green' – that is, immediately after flowering – than to plant the dormant tubers in winter. Alternatively, in late winter some nurseries offer pots of aconites in bud for immediate planting; although these are comparatively expensive, they usually grow away successfully and are a good way of starting an early carpet of gold. *DL*

WINTER CHECKLIST

❦ To avoid needle drop, spray live trees with proprietary non-inflammable Christmas tree spray and keep them cool and moist. 'Harden off' and put them outside after Twelfth Night. Repot in spring and water in summer for re-use next year.

❦ Make a fuss of your houseplants. Move African violets in to more light to keep them flowering. Clean foliage pot plants with damp cotton wool, and 'mist' tropical plants to keep the air humid.

❦ Spring bulbs 'forced' in pots for indoor use perform best if left outside till the flower buds show their true colour; then keep them in a cool room. Plant them out in the garden after flowering.

❦ Send for seed catalogues from the big seed firms – the range available by mail order is much bigger than sold in garden centres. Order early as some varieties may be in short supply.

❦ Clean heated propagators and sow herbaceous perennials to flower this summer. Also slow house and conservatory plants such as the bird of paradise flower (file and soak large hard seeds).

❦ Sow seed of hardy trees, shrubs and alpines on receipt; cover the seed to its own depth with grit and stand pots outdoors as they need a cold spell before germination takes place.

❦ Take advantage of the lull in outdoor work; gardening societies and local groups of specialist societies meet for lectures, plant sales and socials over the winter (details from local libraries).

❦ Dig vacant ground adding organic matter (garden compost or well-rotted manure), if the soil is not too wet. Turn the soil over often so birds can feed on soil pests like wireworm.

❦ Buy Christmas cards and postal gifts from one of the gardening charities' catalogues, or support a garden-oriented one like the Gardeners' Royal Benevolent Society or Royal Society for the Protection of Birds. *SP*

INSTANT WINTER COLOUR
Make good use of 'throw-away' pot
plants; cineraria, exacum, calceolaria
and pot chrysanths for instant winter
colour indoors, and also, decorated with
ribbons, as emergency gifts.

NOTES

GARDENER'S TIP

From early spring onwards, a fortnightly liquid feed will help winter containers to give an impressive display. Sometimes the surface of the compost can become compacted, and food and water will run off rather than soaking in. If this happens, stir it up with an old table fork or house-plant fork. This will improve the appearance and facilitate water and food penetration.

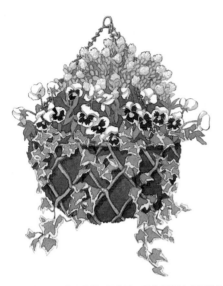

WINTER CARE FOR CONTAINERS

To get a good display of spring flowers in containers, your hanging baskets, tubs and windowboxes should be checked over regularly to ensure the plants are in tip-top condition.

Containers standing on the patio or other paving can become waterlogged if roots block the drainage holes. This can be cured if the holes in the base of the pots are bored out with a piece of cane – any surplus water will soon drain away before plant roots and bulbs start to rot.

Make sure winter containers do not dry out. In windy weather they can soon become dehydrated. The compost should be damp but not saturated; be prepared to water regularly if they start to look dry.

If winter pansies suddenly start to deteriorate, check the base of the stems. The chances are that they are infested with aphids – these should be sprayed with an insecticide immediately, or you could lose them all.

However well you look after your winter containers, in hard spells some plants are likely to die. In early spring your local garden centre should have pots of spring bedding – pansies, forget-me-nots, polyanthus and double daisies – and dwarf bulbs such as crocus, miniature narcissi and botanical tulips, which can be popped in to add colour and revitalize the container, and remind you that spring is on the way. *DL*

USEFUL ADDRESSES

A

Alpine Garden Society
E.M. Upward, The A.G.S. Centre, Avonbank,
Pershore, Worcs WR10 3JP

Arboricultural Association
Ampfield House, Ampfield, Near Romsey,
Hants SO51 9PA

Auricula and Primula Society
National Midland and West Section:
P.G. Ward, 6 Lawson Close, Saltford, Bristol BS18 3LB

Northern Section:
D. Hadfield, 146 Queen's Road, Cheadle,
Cheshire SX8 5HY

Southern Section:
L.E. Wigley, 67 Warnham Court Road,
Carshalton Beeches, Surrey SM5 3ND

B

Begonia Society, National
E. Catterall, 7 Springwood Close, Thurgoland,
Sheffield S30 7AB

Bonsai Association, British
J. White, Inglenook, 36 McCarthy Way, Wokingham,
Berks RG11 4UA

Botanical Society of the British Isles
c/o Dept of Botany, The Natural History Museum,
Cromwell Road, London SW7 5BD

Brogdale Horticultural Trust
Brogdale Road, Faversham, Kent ME13 8XZ

C

Cactus and Succulent Society, British
E.A. Harris, 49 Chestnut Glen, Hornchurch,
Essex RM12 4HL

Camellia Society, International
H.Short, 41 Galveston Road, East Putney,
London SW15 2RZ

Carnation Society, British National
Mrs P. Dimond, 3 Canberra Close, Hornchurch,
Essex RM12 5TR

Carnivorous Plant Society
S. Cottell, 1 Orchard Close, Ringwood,
Hants GH24 1LP

Chrysanthemum Society, National
Unit 8, Amber Business Village, Amber Close,
Amington, Tamworth, Staffs B77 4RP

Clematis Society, British
Mrs B. Risdon, The Tropical Bird Gardens, Rode,
Near Bath, Somerset BA3 6QW

Cottage Garden Society
Mrs C. Tordoff, 5 Nixon Close, Thornhilll, Dewsbury,
W. Yorks WF12 0JA

Cyclamen Society
P. Moore, Tile Barn House, Standen Street,
Iden Green, Benenden, Kent TN17 4LB

D

Daffodil Society
D. Barnes, 32 Montgomery Avenue, Sheffield S7 1NZ

Dahlia Society, National
E.H. Collins, 19 Sunnybank, Marlow, Bucks SL7 3BL

Delphinium Society
R.J. Joslyn, 5 Woodfield Avenue, Carshalton Beeches,
Surrey SM5 3JB

E

European Palm Society
c/o The Palm Centre, 563 Upper Richmond Road,
West London SW14 7ED

F

Forestry Commission
231 Corstorphine Road,
Edinburgh EH12 7AT

Fruit Group of The Royal Horticultural Society
Mrs M. Sweetingham, Royal Horticultural Society,
Vincent Square,
London SW1P 2PE

Fuchsia Society, British
R. Williams, 20 Brodawel, Hannon, Llanelli,
Dyfed SA14 6BJ

G

Garden History Society
Hon. Membership Secretary, 5 The Knoll,
Hereford HR1 1RU

Gardeners' Royal Benevolent Society
Bridge House, 139 Kingston Road, Leatherhead,
Surrey KT22 7NT

Gardening for the Disabled Trust
The Freight, Cranbrook,
Kent TN17 3PG

Geranium Society, British and European
Mrs D.P. Codling, 56 Shrigley Road, Higher Poynton,
Cheshire SK12 1TF

Gladiolus Society, British
Nigel Coe, 24 The Terrace, Mayfield, Ashbourne,
Derbyshire DE6 2JL

H

Hardy Plant Society
Mrs P. Adams, Little Orchard, Great Comberton,
Near Pershore, Worcs WR10 3DP

Heather Society
Mrs A. Small, Denbeigh, All Saints Road,
Creeting St Mary, Ipswich, Suffolk IP6 8PJ

Hebe Society
G. Scoble, Rosemergy, Hain Walk, St Ives
Cornwall TR26 2AF

Henry Doubleday Research Association
Ryton Organic Gardens, Coventry CV8 3LG

Herb Society
134 Buckingham Palace Road, London SW1W 9SA

Horticultural Therapy
Goulds Ground, Vallis Way, Frome
Somerset BA11 3DW

Horticultural Trades Association
19 High Street, Theale, Berks RG7 5AH

Hosta and Hemerocallis Society, British
R. Bowden, Cleave House, Sticklepath, Okehampton,
Devon EX20 2NN

I

Institute of Horticulture
80 Vincent Square, London SW1P 2PE

Iris Society, British
T.R.P. Maynard, 43 Sea Lane, Goring-by-Sea,
Worthing, West Sussex BN12 4QD

Ivy Society, British
Mrs B. Hutchin, 14 Holly Grove, Huyton,
Merseyside L36 4JA

J

Japanese Garden Society
M.L. Dickinson, 45 Moorland Drive, Abbott's Lodge,
Runcorn, Cheshire WA7 6HL

L

Lily Group of The Royal Horticultural Society
Dr Ian Boyd, 14 Marshalls Way, Wheathampstead,
St Alban's, Herts AL4 8HY

M

Mammillaria Society
C.P. Baker, 22 Stirling Road, Chichester,
West Sussex PO19 2ES

Museum of Garden History
The Tradescant Trust, Lambeth Palace Road,
London SE1 7LB

N

**National Association of Flower Arrangement
Societies of Great Britain**
21 Denbigh Street,
London SW1V 2HF

**National Council for the Conservation of
Plants and Gardens**
The Pines, RHS Garden, Wisley, Woking,
Surrey GU23 6QB

National Gardens Scheme
Hatchlands Park, East Clandon, Guildford
Surrey GU4 7RT

**National Society of Allotment and Leisure
Gardeners Ltd**
Odell House, Hunters Road, Corby,
Northants NN17 1JE

National Trust
36 Queen Anne's Gate, London SW1H 9AS

National Trust for Scotland
5 Charlotte Square, Edinburgh EH2 4DU

Northern Horticultural Society
The Administrator, Harlow Carr Botanical Gardens,
Crag Lane, Harrogate HG3 1QB

O

Orchid Council, British
A.J. Hainsworth, 52 Weasle Lane, Thelwall,
Cheshire WA4 3JR

Orchid Society, Scottish
Mr C. Hind, 20 Ancrum Road, Dundee DD2 2HZ

P

Pelargonium and Geranium Society, British
Carol & Ron Helyar, 134 Montrose Avenue, Welling,
Kent DA16 2QY

Pot Leek Society, National
A. Waite, 8 Nelson Avenue, Nelson Village, Cramlington, Northumberland

Pteridological Society, British
A.R. Busby, 16 Kirby Corner Road, Canley, Coventry CV4 8GD

R

RHS Rhododendron, Camellia and Magnolia Group
Mrs J.M.Warren, Netherton, Buckland Monachorum, Yelverton, Devon PL20 7NL

Rose, Carnation and Sweet Pea Society, North of England
J. Ramm, 94 Hedgehope Road, Westerhope, Newcastle upon Tyne NE5 4LA

Royal Caledonian Horticultural Society
Dr Philip Crooks, 21 Newbattle Abbey Crescent, Dalkeith EH22 3LN

Royal Horticultural Society
80 Vincent Square, London SW1P 2PE

Royal Horticultural Society of Ireland
Swanbrook House, Bloomfield Avenue, Donnybrook, Dublin 4

Royal National Rose Society
K.J. Grapes, Chiswell Green, St Albans, Herts AL2 3NR

S

Saintpaulia and Houseplant Society
33 Church Road, Newbury Park, Ilford, Essex IG2 7ET

Scotland's Gardens Scheme
31 Castle Terrace, Edinburgh EH1 2EL

Scottish Rock Garden Club
Dr Jan Boyd, Groom's Cottage Flat, Kirklands, Ancrum, Jedburgh TD8 6UJ

Sedum Society
Prof. Mavis Doyle, OBE, 12 Langdale Road, Gateshead NE9 5RN

Sempervivum Society
11 Wingle Tye Road, Burgess Hill, West Sussex RH15 9HR

Soil Association
86 Colston Street, Bristol BS1 5BB

Sweet Pea Society, National
J.R.F. Bishop, 3 Chalk Farm Road, Stokenchurch, High Wycombe, Bucks HP14 3TB

Sweet Pea, Rose and Carnation Society, Scottish National
Mrs J. Reid, 72 West George Street, Coatbridge, Lanarkshire ML5 2DD

V

Vegetable Society, National
I. Garland, 56 Waun-y-Groes Avenue, Rhiwbina, Cardiff, South Glamorgan

Viola and Pansy Society, National
Tom Pitt, 28 Carisbrooke Road, Edgbaston, Birmingham B17 8NW

W

Wild Flower Society
68 Outwoods Road, Loughborough, Leics LE11 3LY

Worshipful Company of Gardeners
N.G.S. Gray, 25 Luke Street, London EC2A 4AR

A
aconite, winter 166
Algerian iris 166
Allium 86
alpines 42, 110, 129, 168
annuals 18, 129, 131
arbours 41
autumn colour 115

B
bark, coloured 139
barrels 75
beans 26, 49, 63
bedding plants 18, 25, 49, 88, 102, 129
berries 138, 139
biennials 88, 131
brassicas 49
bulbs 46, 82, 86, 110, 129, 168

C
cabbages 88
chicory 149
Chillington hoes 140
Christmas trees 168
Clematis armandii 14
climbing plants 41, 63
colour, autumn 115
containers 163
  cuttings 22
  half-barrels 75
  hanging baskets 34, 118–19
  strawberries 66
  strawberry pots 99
  troughs 42
  watering 88
  windowboxes 134–5
  in winter 129, 170–1
Cosmos atrosanguineus 29
cuttings 22

D
dead-heading 80, 88
digging 91, 168
diseases 60–1

E
eccentricity 59
Eranthis hyemalis 166
evergreens 104, 138

F
flowering lawns 54
forcing plants 149
forks 64, 121
French beans 26, 49
fruit 88, 116

G
gentians 95
grass seed 49, 76

greenhouse 49, 129
ground cover 126

H
hanging baskets 34, 118–19
heathers 146
hedges 88, 104, 137
herbaceous perennials 49, 63, 113, 168
herbs 72–3, 125, 144–5
Hesperis matronalis 71
hoes 33, 45, 64, 140
houseplants 52, 168, 169
hyacinths 82
hydrangeas 20

I
irises 88, 96, 166

J
Jasminum nudiflorum 159

K
knot gardens 58

L
labels 164
lawns 49, 54, 76, 88, 129
leaf mould 132
leaf sweepers, electric 121
lilies 86

M
meadows 54
measuring sticks 33
moisture-loving plants 38
mulches 16–17, 45

N
nasturtiums 79

O
onions, ornamental 86

P
Parthenocissus henryana 122
pelargoniums 22, 88
perennials 96–7, 131
pests 60
pitchforks 121
plums 92
ponds 150
potagers 153
potatoes 36, 37, 49, 88
power tools 100
pruning 21, 104, 129
pruning saws 140
pumpkins 107

R
rhubarb 149

rock gardens 110
roses 49, 80, 102, 126, 129
runner beans 26, 49, 63

S
salad leaves 12–13
scent 143
seakale 149
seedlings 25
seeds 85, 109, 156, 168
sheep shears 64
shrubs: planting 160
  plants beneath 46
  pruning 21
  wildlife 155
slugs 30
soil 91, 168
spades 33, 140
staking 62–3
strawberries 66, 88, 89
strawberry pots 99

T
tender plants 129
tools 33, 64, 100, 121, 140
topiary 104
trees: planting 160
  seeds 109, 168
  staking 62–3
  wildlife 155
  windbreaks 137
trellises 137
Tropaeolum 79
troughs 42
tulips 57
turf 76

V
vegetables: forcing 149
  potagers 153
  seeds 85
virus-free plants 61

W
watering 69, 88
weed forks, long-handled 64
weeds 45
wildlife 150, 155
windbreaks 137
windowboxes 134–5